30-DAY LEADERSHIP CHALLENGE

PRACTICAL LESSONS TO BUILD CONFIDENCE INFLUENCE IMPACT

MICHELLE POURCHOT

CONTENTS

PREFACE

Writing a book has been a dream of mine for many years. I've always loved leading, helping others, and watching people grow and learn. To me, one of the greatest privileges of leadership is seeing the potential in others and helping them realize it for themselves.

Over the years, I've read countless incredible leadership books, each offering valuable insights that have shaped and inspired me. Those experiences fueled my desire to create something of my own. Having been in a leadership role for 20 years, I know time is something we don't have an abundance of, so I wanted to write a leadership book that would get straight to the point.

This isn't a book you simply read once and set aside. It's meant to be a practical tool, something you can pull out whenever you want to focus on a specific area of your leadership, even if you're not doing the whole 30-day challenge.

Inside these pages, I've pulled together the lessons, habits, and mindsets that I believe are the most critical for any leader. These are the areas that have guided me throughout my leadership journey, and I'm excited to pass them on to you.

More than anything, I hope this book is practical and encouraging, something you turn to when you need a boost, a reminder, or a fresh idea. I hope it inspires you to keep growing, lead with heart, and never underestimate the difference you can make.

Thank you for letting me be a small part of your leadership journey. I truly hope you enjoy the book, and that it helps you grow, lead, and live with even greater purpose.

INTRODUCTION

What is the 30-Day Leadership Challenge, and who is it for?

This book is for anyone who wants to take their leadership to the next level. It is for people ready to roll up their sleeves and work. This is not a book you pick up and read in one sitting. Think of it more as a "work in progress" journey. For some, it will take 30 days, and others may need to allow a few days to practice the focus principle. The goal is not to fit it all in 30 days but rather to challenge yourself, push beyond your comfort zone, and GROW!

Becoming a great leader is not about having natural talent, although some leaders do. It is not about years of experience because I have seen first-year leaders be more effective than those with 20 years of experience. You may think you can't be an effective leader because you are not an extrovert, but the truth is some of the most intuitive leaders are introverts.

If you desire to grow and learn, then you have picked up the right book to get you started and have taken the first step to becoming a better leader. The next step is taking action and stepping out of your comfort zone to see the change unfold. Change is not easy. It will take hard work and your commitment to change, not just on the easy days but also on the hard ones.

Each topic has been carefully selected and plays a role in becoming a well-rounded leader.

Why 30 days?

Habits take time to form, but committing to just one focused leadership practice each day lays the foundation for long-term growth. No one becomes a great leader overnight, but if you take this book to heart and apply the principles, you will be a more effective leader 30 days from now. Only you can drive the change! The tools are contained in this book; you decide what you will do with them.

The layout of this book will help you build leadership skills in a structured way, allowing you to integrate the lessons into your daily life, no matter where you are in your leadership journey.

Your 30-day journey is divided into three sections; each serves as a foundation for the following: Leading Yourself-Leading Others-Leading for Impact.

Part 1: Leading Yourself (Days 1-10)

Before you can effectively lead others, you must first lead yourself. The first ten days focus on self-leadership: defining your leadership vision, becoming self-aware, and learning the importance of emotional intelligence, confidence, decision-making, and other foundational self-leadership skills.

Part 2: Leading Others (Days 11-20)

After you learn to lead yourself, you are ready to lead others. Days 11-20 focus on influence, connection, and service. In this section, you'll learn how to communicate effectively, give and receive feedback, and build strong, trusting relationships. You'll learn the importance of active listening, coaching vs. managing, handling conflict gracefully, and fostering a thriving work culture that inspires others.

Part 3: Leading for Impact (Days 21-30)

During the final 10 days of your leadership challenge, you'll focus on leading in a way that leaves a lasting impact. Leadership is not just about the present moment; it's about creating a legacy. You'll learn how to adapt your leadership in a changing world, build resilience, manage your energy, lead through difficult situations, and leave a lasting mark on the world. You'll learn tools to avoid burnout, the power of storytelling, navigating tough conversations, and defining the leadership legacy you want to leave.

What to Expect Each Day

Each chapter follows a simple yet powerful structure:

- **A Leadership Principle:** The key concept for the day.

- **A Case Study or Practical Example** of a leader who embodies this principle.

- **A Practical Exercise:** A challenge or activity for you to apply what you've learned that day.

- **Final Principle:** One overarching lesson to carry with you beyond the day's challenge.

- **Action Steps for that Day:** Clear, simple takeaways to reinforce your leadership growth.

Remember, your journey is about growth, not perfection. Some days will challenge you more than others. Some lessons will resonate immediately, while others may take time to sink in. The key is to keep going.

Your Leadership Challenge Starts Now

You are here because you want to grow. You are here because you know leadership isn't just for a select few; it's for those willing to step up, take action, and inspire change. This book is your blueprint for transformation.

Do you accept the 30-Day Challenge?

Are you ready to lead?

If so, let's begin!

As you read the 30-Day Leadership Challenge, you will encounter reflection questions, strategies to try, and daily action steps. I have created the **30-Day Leadership Challenge Workbook** to enhance your learning and align with the book's content. This workbook provides space for you to write down your thoughts and explore the lessons in more depth. It brings the book to life, allowing you not only to read but also to put pen to paper, make commitments, and create habits that have a lasting impact and real change. The companion workbook can be found through the same retailer where you purchased this book.

PART 1

DAYS 1-10: LEADING YOURSELF

DAY 1: DEFINE YOUR LEADERSHIP VISION

WHAT KIND OF LEADER DO YOU WANT TO BE?

Fresh out of college, Lisa got her first leadership role at a fast-growing tech startup. She was excited but nervous. She was ready to jump into the position and eager to prove herself. However, within weeks, she found herself overwhelmed. Decisions had to be made, and her team looked to her for answers. Then, self-doubt began to creep in.

One afternoon, after a particularly frustrating team meeting, her mentor sat her down and said, *"You're trying to lead without knowing where you're going. Leadership isn't about just managing tasks; it's about having a vision. What kind of leader do you want to be?"*

Leadership starts with who you are, not just what you do.

She had never considered leadership that way before. She had always assumed it was about getting things done. Then, she began to realize that leadership starts with **who you are, not just what you do**.

Whether you're stepping into leadership for the first time or refining your skills, you must start with clarity. **What kind of leader do you want to be?** The answer to that question will shape every decision you make.

Leadership Without Vision is Like Driving Without a Destination

Leadership is not a job title; it's a responsibility. Some of the most influential leaders in history, from Martin Luther King Jr. to Mother Teresa, did not lead because they held a position of authority. They led because they had a clear vision of what they wanted to achieve. Without a clear vision, leadership becomes reactive; constantly responding to challenges without a guiding purpose. With a vision, leadership becomes intentional, and every action aligns with a greater mission.

Author and leadership expert John C. Maxwell once said:

> *"People buy into the leader before they buy into the vision."* [1]

This means that before others trust your leadership, you must first trust yourself—and that begins with defining your vision.

Case Study: Simon Sinek's "Why" Principle

Few leadership speakers have had as much impact in recent years as Simon Sinek, the author of *Start With Why*. His research on effective leadership boils down to a simple yet powerful idea: Great leaders don't start with *what* they do or *how* they do it—they start with *why* they do it. Sinek uses a framework for what he calls the Golden Circle [2], which has three layers:

- **WHAT:** What you do (your job, your tasks, your responsibilities).

- **HOW:** How you do it (your processes, strategies, methods).

- **WHY:** Why you do it (your purpose, your core belief, your impact).

Most people and organizations start from the outside in; they can explain what they do and how they do it, but they struggle to articulate why.

The world's best leaders, however, start with **why,** and that's what makes them compelling.

Apple's "Why" in Leadership

In Simon Sinek's famous Ted Talk, he uses the following example from Apple to make his point. "Consider Apple. If they marketed themselves like most companies, they would say: '*We make great computers (WHAT). They're beautifully designed and easy to use (HOW). Want to buy one?*' That's not inspiring. Instead, Apple starts with their why: '*Everything we do challenges the status quo (WHY). We believe in thinking differently. We design products that are beautifully made and easy to use (HOW). We just happen to make great computers (WHAT). Want to buy one?*' This is why Apple doesn't just have customers, it has fans. Their leadership vision is clear, compelling, and inspiring."[3]

Exercise: Craft Your Leadership Vision Statement

Now, let's put your vision into words. A **Leadership Vision Statement** is a simple, powerful declaration of the kind of leader you want to be. If you can't define why you lead, it's hard to inspire others to follow.

Step 1: Answer These Reflection Questions

- **What values define you as a leader?** (Integrity, innovation, service, resilience, etc.)

- **Who do you want to impact?** (Your team, organization, students, customers, community?)

- **What leadership qualities do you admire in others?** (Empathy, decisiveness, humility, vision?)

- **What do you want people to say about your leadership 10 years from now?**

Step 2: Write Your Leadership Vision Statement

Use this formula as a guide:

"I am a leader who [core belief]. I achieve this by [key action or approach] so that [impact or goal]."

Example 1: "I am a leader who empowers others by fostering trust and open communication, so that my team feels confident to take risks and grow."

Example 2: "I am a leader who leads with integrity and courage, making tough decisions with honesty to build a culture of respect and accountability."

Once you've written your statement, say it out loud. Does it resonate? If it doesn't, refine it until it feels authentic.

Practical Example: How One Leader's Vision Changed Everything

In 2008, Rebecca stepped into the role of manager. She was only 20, and the team was already falling apart. Morale was low, turnover was high, and people dreaded coming to work. She was unsure where to start, so she decided to **define her leadership vision** first instead of focusing solely on numbers.

Her mission? *"I am a leader who creates an environment where people feel valued, inspired, and supported. I achieve this by fostering trust, giving clear direction, and celebrating small wins so that my team feels empowered to do their best work."*

After defining her leadership vision, Rebecca shared it with her team. Over time, things slowly began to change. She started listening more, acknowledging contributions, and setting clear expectations. Within a year, engagement scores soared, and her department became one of the company's top-performing teams. Rebecca's story proves that **leadership is not about authority; it's about clarity.**

Final Principle: Your Leadership Vision is a Living Document

Defining your leadership vision isn't a **one-time task;** it's a **continuous journey**. Your vision may evolve as you grow, learn, and face new challenges.

Leadership expert Warren Bennis once said:

> *"Becoming a leader is synonymous with becoming yourself. It is precisely that simple, and it is also that difficult."* [4]

As you embark on this 30-day leadership challenge, remember:

1. Your leadership vision is the compass that guides your journey.

2. Your "why" drives your decisions.

3. Leadership is a journey, not a destination.

Your Action Steps for Today:
- Write your Leadership Vision Statement.
- Share it with a trusted colleague or mentor.
- Post it somewhere visible as a daily reminder.

CONGRATULATIONS! YOU'VE JUST TAKEN THE FIRST STEP IN TRANSFORMING YOUR LEADERSHIP. ARE YOU READY TO LEAD?

DAY 2: THE POWER OF A GROWTH MINDSET

THE FOUNDATION OF LEADERSHIP: YOUR MINDSET

Imagine two leaders facing the same challenge.

Tom struggles when his team fails to meet expectations. Frustrated, he thinks, *"Maybe I'm just not cut out for this. Leadership isn't something I can learn; you either have it or you don't."* With this mindset, he starts playing it safe. He avoids risks, and becomes very defensive when anyone tries to give him feedback.

Steve, on the other hand, sees the same challenge as a learning opportunity. He asks himself, *"What can I do differently next time?"* He understands that leadership is a skill that can be improved with practice. He seeks feedback, tries new approaches, and pushes through difficulties.

What separates these two leaders? **Mindset.**

You must lead yourself before you can lead others effectively, and leadership begins in the mind. How you think about your potential influences every aspect of your leadership. If you believe leadership ability is fixed, you'll avoid challenges, resist growth, and miss opportunities to improve. But if you believe leadership is something that can be developed, you'll embrace challenges, learn from mistakes, and continuously improve.

This distinction between a **fixed mindset** and a **growth mindset** is what separates **average leaders from great leaders**.

Fixed vs. Growth Mindset in Leadership

In Dr. Carol Dweck's book, *Mindset: The New Psychology of Success* [5], she introduced the concept of growth mindset in her groundbreaking research on motivation and learning. She found that people generally fall into one of two categories:

Fixed Mindset

- Believes intelligence, talent, and leadership ability are *innate and unchangeable*.

- Avoids challenges that could lead to failure.

- Feels threatened by feedback or the success of others.

- Prefers to stick with what they already know.

Growth Mindset

- Believes intelligence, talent, and leadership ability *can be developed through effort and learning*.

- Embraces challenges as opportunities for growth.

- Views feedback as a valuable tool for improvement.

- Seeks out new experiences and continuous learning.

How Mindset Affects Leadership

A fixed mindset leader tends to:

- Resist feedback because they see it as criticism rather than guidance.

- Micromanage because they don't trust others to improve.

- Avoid tough decisions for fear of failure.

- Struggle with resilience when facing setbacks.

A **growth mindset leader tends to:**

- Encourage feedback because they view it as a learning tool.

- Develop their team by allowing autonomy and learning from mistakes.

- Take bold action and adapt to challenges.

- Demonstrate resilience, knowing failure is a stepping stone to success.

John C. Maxwell, one of the world's top leadership experts, put it best:

"Growth inside fuels growth outside." [6]

If you want to inspire a high-performing team, you must first adopt a high-growth mindset.

Practical Example: How Mindset Transformed a Struggling Leader

Mark had always been a high achiever. He graduated top of his class, landed a great job, and quickly climbed the ranks. But when he was promoted to team leader, things changed.

Things had always come easily for him, but his once-reliable instincts seemed to fail him. He struggled to delegate and often second-guessed his team's abilities. He took things personally when they went wrong. He started to question if he had what it takes to be a leader.

One day, his mentor pulled him aside and said something that changed his trajectory: *"Mark, leadership isn't about knowing everything; it's about learning everything. The best leaders aren't born; they're built."*

That conversation flipped a switch in Mark. He realized that his struggles were not a sign of failure but a part of growth. He started to approach leadership like a skill rather than a test of his ability. He actively sought feedback, read leadership books, and took small risks. Slowly, his confidence grew. Within a year, Mark had transformed his team's performance because he had transformed his own mindset first.

The takeaway? You are not "bad" or "good" at leadership. You are simply in the process of becoming better.

Exercise: Identify and Reframe Your Limiting Beliefs

Leaders with a **fixed mindset** often hold limiting beliefs. They are often deep-seated thoughts that prevent you from growing. These beliefs might sound like:

- *"I'm just not a natural leader."*

- *"I hate public speaking, so I'll never be good at it."*

- *"I don't have the right personality to be an inspiring leader."*

- *"If I make a mistake, people will lose confidence in me."*

To develop a growth mindset, you need to reframe these beliefs.

Step 1: Write Down Your Limiting Beliefs

Take a moment to reflect: What doubts do you have about your leadership abilities? Write them down.

Step 2: Challenge Those Beliefs

For each limiting belief you wrote down, ask yourself:

- *Is this really true?*

- *What evidence do I have to support or contradict it?*

- *Has anyone in history overcome this same challenge?*

Step 3: Reframe with a Growth Mindset

Now, rewrite each limiting belief as a growth mindset statement.

Instead of: *"I'm just not a natural leader."*

Try: *"Leadership is a skill, and I can develop it with practice."*

Instead of: *"I hate public speaking, so I'll never be good at it."*

Try: *"Public speaking is uncomfortable now, but with practice, I can improve."*

Instead of: *"I don't have the right personality to be an inspiring leader."*

Try: *"Different leadership styles work for different people. I will lead in a way that fits my strengths."*

Instead of: *"If I make a mistake, people will lose confidence in me."*

Try: *"Mistakes are part of leadership. Owning them and learning from them will actually build my team's trust."*

By shifting how you frame challenges, you empower yourself to grow.

The Research: How a Growth Mindset Transforms Performance

Dr. Carol Dweck's research shows that people with a growth mindset are more likely to succeed; not because they're smarter or more talented, but because they're more willing to learn.

One of her studies followed students who struggled in school. Those with a fixed mindset believed their intelligence was permanent, so they gave up easily. But those with a growth mindset believed they could improve with effort, and they outperformed their peers as a result.

The same principle applies to leadership. Leaders who believe they can improve are the ones who do improve.

As Dweck puts it: *"Becoming is better than being."* [7]

Final Principle: Leadership is a Learning Process

If there's one thing to take away from today's lesson, it's this:

Leadership is not about perfection-it's about progress.

Every great leader struggled at some point. But they didn't let those struggles define them. They adopted a **growth mindset**, embraced feedback, and committed to learning.

Your Action Steps for Today:

- Identify **one** limiting belief that's holding you back.

- Reframe it using a growth mindset statement.

- Commit to one small action that pushes you outside your comfort zone.

ARE YOU READY TO GROW?

Day 3: The Power of Self-Awareness

The Mirror of Leadership

Consider two leaders walking into a team meeting.

Larry is frustrated. His team missed a deadline, and he immediately started blaming external factors, market conditions, unmotivated employees, and unclear client requests. After a few minutes of displaying his frustration in front of his team, he could sense the tension in the room rising and noticed the team was beginning to withdraw.

Michael, facing the same missed deadline, takes a different approach. He asks himself, "*What role did I play in missing the deadline?*" He reflects on whether he set clear expectations, provided support, and communicated effectively with his team. Instead of blaming his team and other factors, he takes ownership of what went wrong and uses the situation as a learning opportunity.

What separates these two leaders? **Self-awareness.**

Leadership isn't just about inspiring others; it's about knowing yourself first. The best leaders understand their strengths, weaknesses, triggers, and blind spots. **They don't just lead by instinct; they lead with intention.**

Why Self-Awareness is Essential for Leadership

Dr. Tasha Eurich, an organizational psychologist, conducted a multi-year study on self-awareness and leadership. Her research found that: **95% of people think they are self-aware, but only 10-15% actually are.**[8]

That means most leaders **believe** they understand themselves, but their perception doesn't match reality. That is pretty crazy, right? I think I'm self-aware, but maybe not. Do you think you are self-aware?

Why is being self-aware as a leader important? Because self-aware leaders are more effective because they:

- Make better decisions by understanding their biases.

- Communicate more clearly because they recognize their own emotions and triggers.

- Build stronger teams by acknowledging their weaknesses and empowering others.

- Handle stress better because they recognize when they need to reset.

As Peter Drucker, the father of modern management, said:

"You cannot manage other people unless you manage yourself first."[9]

The Two Types of Self-Awareness

Self-awareness isn't just about introspection; it's about seeing yourself accurately from multiple perspectives.

1. Internal Self-Awareness *(How well you understand yourself)*: This includes your values, strengths, weaknesses, habits, and triggers. Leaders with strong internal self-awareness are more confident and authentic because they lead in alignment with who they truly are.

For example, leaders who know they struggle with delegation make a conscious effort to empower their team rather than micromanage.

2. External Self-Awareness *(How well you understand how others see you)*: This is your ability to see yourself through the eyes of your team, peers, and mentors. Leaders who lack external self-awareness often don't realize how their actions affect others.

Example: A leader who thinks they are approachable but rarely invites feedback may not realize their team feels intimidated or unheard.

Great leaders develop **both** types of self-awareness to close the gap between how they see themselves and how others experience their leadership.

Practical Example: A CEO's Self-Awareness Wake-Up Call

Debbie was the CEO of a fast-growing startup and liked to think of herself as a visionary. But the truth is, her team had a different perspective. In a leadership survey, they frequently described her as being distant and hard to approach. At first, Debbie was offended and resisted the feedback. She said to herself, "*That's not true! I have an open-door policy.*" But then she took a step back, and after considering the feedback from her survey, she realized the issue:

- She was **always rushing** between meetings.

- She **rarely made eye contact** when people spoke.

- She **seemed distracted** during one-on-ones.

The result? Her team felt like she wasn't fully present.

Debbie committed to improving her **external self-awareness**. She started blocking out time for genuine conversations, gave her full attention during meetings, and actively sought feedback. Within a few months, her team reported they were feeling **more connected and valued;** all because she was willing to see herself through their eyes.

The takeaway? Leadership isn't just about how you think you show up; it's about how others experience you.

Exercise: Your Leadership Self-Awareness Audit

To improve self-awareness, you need honest reflection and external feedback.

Step 1: Self-Reflection

Take a few minutes to answer the following:

- *What are my three greatest leadership strengths?*

- *What leadership behaviors or habits do I struggle with?*

- *What situations trigger frustration or stress in me?*

- *How do I typically react under pressure?*

Step 2: Ask for Feedback

Choose three trusted colleagues, employees, or mentors (not someone who will tell you what you want to hear) and ask them:

- *What's one strength you see in my leadership?*

- *What's one area where I could improve?*

- *How do you experience my leadership style?*

This can be humbling, but great leaders **seek truth over comfort**.

Step 3: Identify Blind Spots

Compare your self-reflection with the feedback you receive. If there's a gap, don't get defensive-get curious. Ask yourself:

- *Why might there be a difference between how I see myself and how others see me?*

- *What small adjustments could I make to align my impact with my intention?*

Self-awareness isn't about perfection; it's about **progress**.

The Research: Why Self-Aware Leaders Perform Better

Dr. Eurich's research on self-awareness found that leaders who actively develop **both internal and external self-awareness** experience:

- Higher job satisfaction and effectiveness

- Better team performance and communication

- Stronger decision-making skills

Leaders who regularly seek feedback and reflect on their leadership style are consistently rated as the most effective. As Dr. Eurich puts it:

"Self-awareness is the secret ingredient of successful leadership."[10]

The best leaders don't just assume they're doing well; they check in with their team, adjust, and grow.

Final Principle: Self-Awareness is a Leadership Superpower

If you want to become the kind of leader who earns trust, builds strong teams, and inspires action, you must first develop the ability to see yourself clearly.

- Self-aware leaders don't react-they respond.

- They don't blame-they reflect.

- They don't guess-they ask.

Your Action Steps For Today

- Complete the **Self-Awareness Audit** (reflection + feedback).

- Identify **one blind spot** and commit to a small improvement.

- Ask at least **one person for honest feedback** on your leadership.

ARE YOU READY TO LEVEL UP YOUR LEADERSHIP SELF-AWARENESS?

DAY 4: MASTERING EMOTIONAL INTELLIGENCE

THE HEART OF LEADERSHIP

Imagine two managers handling a difficult situation:

Emily is results-driven but emotionally detached. When an employee comes to her, expressing that she is overwhelmed with work, Emily replies, *"Everyone's busy, just get it done."* After the conversation, the employee leaves feeling unheard, unmotivated, and disengaged.

Carol is also results-driven but listens, acknowledges the challenge, and responds with, *"I understand this is a lot. Let's break it down together and see where I can better support you."* The employee leaves feeling valued and ready to tackle the challenge.

What's the difference? **Emotional Intelligence (EI).**

In today's world, IQ alone isn't enough to lead effectively. Research shows that leaders with high emotional intelligence outperform those who rely solely on logic and technical skills.[11]

What is Emotional Intelligence?

Dr. Daniel Goleman, the psychologist who popularized **emotional intelligence**, defines it as: *"The ability to recognize, understand, and manage our own emotions while also recognizing, understanding, and influencing the emotions of others."* [12]

EI consists of 5 core components:

1. **Self-Awareness** – Recognizing your emotions and their impact.

2. **Self-Regulation** – Managing emotional reactions in a productive way.

3. **Motivation** – Staying driven and resilient in the face of challenges.

4. **Empathy** – Understanding and relating to others' emotions.

5. **Social Skills** – Building strong relationships and influencing others.

Great leaders develop all five components, creating teams that are more engaged, connected, and high-performing.

As Maya Angelou wisely said:

"People will forget what you said, people will forget what you did, but people will never forget how you made them feel." [13]

Why Emotional Intelligence is the #1 Leadership Skill

Research proves that emotional intelligence drives leadership success:

- Harvard Business Review found that EI is responsible for nearly 90% of the difference between high performers and their peers.[14]

- A study by TalentSmart showed that leaders with high EI make better decisions 80% of the time. [15]

- Gallup research found that leaders who display empathy and emotional intelligence retain employees at significantly higher rates. [16]

In other words, EI isn't just a *nice-to-have;* it's essential to being an effective leader.

According to research:

- EI is the strongest predictor of leadership success, more than IQ or technical skills. [17]

- Employees are 4x more likely to stay engaged when led by an emotionally intelligent leader. [18]

- A leader's ability to regulate emotions affects team morale, retention, and overall performance.

The best part is EI isn't fixed; it can be developed.

Practical Example: The Leader Who Turned a Team Around

Paul was a talented sales director. He knew the business inside and out but struggled to connect with his team. When people underperformed, he immediately focused on numbers instead of the root problem. His employees described him as intimidating and unapproachable.

One day, Paul's top salesperson unexpectedly resigned. When he asked why, she told him, *"I never felt like you cared about me, just my results."* That was a wake-up call for Paul.

Paul committed to developing his emotional intelligence:

- He started **actively listening** instead of just instructing.

- He learned to **ask more questions** instead of jumping to conclusions.

- He made **one-on-one check-ins** about more than just performance; he asked about their well-being and personal growth.

Within a few months, his team transformed. Employee satisfaction increased, turnover decreased, and performance skyrocketed; not because he changed his expertise, but because he changed his leadership approach.

Exercise: Strengthening Your Emotional Intelligence

Improving your EI starts with small, intentional actions.

Step 1: Identify Your Emotional Triggers

Think about the last time you felt:

- Frustrated with a colleague or employee

- Defensive in a conversation

- Stressed about a high-pressure situation

Ask yourself:

- *What emotions surfaced?*

- *How did I react?*

- *What could I have done differently?*

Recognizing emotional triggers is the first step to self-regulation.[19]

Step 2: Practice Active Listening

Next time you have a conversation, try this:

- Make eye contact and give your full attention.

- Resist the urge to interrupt or immediately offer advice.

- Reflect back on what you heard (*"It sounds like you're feeling __ because __."*).

This small shift builds **trust, connection, and understanding,** which is the foundation of an emotionally intelligent leader.[20]

Step 3: Strengthen Your Empathy Muscle

Before reacting to a situation, pause and consider the other person's perspective [21]:

- *What pressures are they under?*

- *What emotions might they be experiencing?*

- *How would I feel if I were in their shoes?*

The best leaders lead with understanding, not assumption.

The Research: How EI Boosts Team Performance

A study by Google's Project Oxygen analyzed what makes great leaders stand out. The top result? Emotional intelligence and empathy. [22]

- Teams with empathetic leaders were more innovative and productive.

- Leaders who practiced active listening and emotional support had higher employee retention and satisfaction.

- Organizations led by high-EI executives experienced greater long-term success than those led by IQ-driven, emotionally detached leaders.

As Simon Sinek says:

"Leadership is not about being in charge. It is about taking care of those in your charge." [23]

Final Principle: Emotional Intelligence is Your Competitive Edge

In today's fast-paced world, technical skills alone won't make you a great leader; instead, **your ability to connect, understand, and influence people sets you apart**.

Emotionally intelligent leaders:

- Inspire trust and loyalty.

- Communicate effectively and handle conflict with grace.

- Make people feel valued, seen, and motivated to perform at their best.

Your Action Steps For Today

- Identify **one emotional trigger** and reflect on how to manage it better.

- Practice **active listening** in your next conversation.

- Show **genuine empathy** by considering someone else's perspective before reacting.

ARE YOU READY TO UNLOCK THE FULL POWER OF EMOTIONAL
INTELLIGENCE IN YOUR LEADERSHIP?

DAY 5: THE CONFIDENCE EXPERIMENT

WHERE COURAGE MEETS CONVICTION

"Whether you think you can, or you think you can't-you're right." -
Henry Ford[24]

The role of confidence in leadership is often mistaken for
arrogance, but in reality, it is the foundation of influence,
trust, and leadership presence. A leader who exudes confidence
fosters a sense of security within their team, inspires action,
and is more likely to gain buy-in for their vision. The difference
between a leader who struggles and one who thrives isn't always
intelligence, skill, or experience; it's belief in their own abilities.

Most people are not born with confidence in their leadership
ability (well, some are way too confident in themselves). It's
something you cultivate through deliberate practice. That means
that confidence can be trained and strengthened like a muscle.

The Science Behind Confidence

Dr. Amy Cuddy, a Harvard psychologist and researcher,
introduced the world to the concept of **power posing.** The
idea is that changing your posture can influence your brain

chemistry and, in turn, your confidence levels. Her research demonstrated that standing in a **"high-power pose"** (or what I like to call the Superman pose) for just two minutes could increase testosterone (the dominance hormone) and decrease cortisol (the stress hormone). This physical shift translates into greater self-assurance, improved performance, and stronger leadership presence. [25]

Cuddy's work challenges the belief that confidence is only built from external achievements. Instead, it shows that confidence is also internal, something you can generate within yourself before you ever step into a leadership role.

Exercise: The Confidence Experiment-Power Posing & Positive Self-Talk

Today's challenge involves two simple but powerful techniques:

1. Power Posing: "Fake it till you become it!"

Before walking into any high-stakes situation; a presentation, a tough conversation, or a leadership moment, take **two minutes** in a power pose:

- Stand tall with your feet shoulder-width apart.

- Place your hands on your hips or stretch your arms in a "victory pose" (visualize how Superman stands or someone who just won a race raising hands in victory)

- Keep your chin up and your chest open.

- Hold this pose for **two minutes** before entering the room.

I know it sounds corny, but I promise you, it works because I've used this technique several times! This practice isn't about deception; it's about rewiring your mindset to embrace leadership confidence. As Cuddy famously said:

"Don't fake it till you make it. Fake it till you become it." [26]

Now, I add one additional step to the "power pose." Once I come out of that pose, I visualize myself walking over a line into whatever I am about to do. I tell myself that once I cross this invisible line, I am confident and have what it takes to accomplish whatever I am about to do. The person on the other side of the line has confidence and assurance. Believe it or not, it works!

2. Positive Self-Talk: Your Inner Coach vs. Your Inner Critic

We all have an inner dialogue running in our minds, but too often, that voice is a harsh critic rather than an encouraging coach. Research shows that our thoughts shape our reality—and leaders who master their internal dialogue exude confidence naturally.

It may sound silly, but your challenge is to replace self-doubt with affirmations that reinforce leadership confidence. Throughout the day, whenever self-doubt creeps in, use one of these confidence-boosting statements:

- *"I am a leader, and what I do today matters."*

- *"I am prepared, capable, and ready to handle this challenge."*

- *"I bring value and inspire others through my actions."*

This shift from self-doubt to self-trust is what separates great leaders from those who hold themselves back.

Real-Life Example: Simon Sinek on Confidence and Leadership Influence

Let's look at Simon Sinek again (mentioned on Day 1). He is best known for his book *Start With Why*, which emphasizes that true leadership confidence comes from clarity of purpose, not just external achievements.

In his well-known TED Talk, Simon Sinek emphasizes that self-confidence is a defining trait of effective leaders like Martin Luther King Jr. and Steve Jobs. These leaders built trust not by merely promoting products or ideas, but by being guided by their core purpose, or "why." Their unwavering belief in their ability to create change fostered confidence in others, inspiring them to believe in the leaders' vision and follow their lead.[27]

Leadership confidence isn't about always having the perfect answer. It's about having conviction in your purpose, standing firmly in your values, and making decisions even in uncertain situations.

Practical Story: The Leadership Confidence Shift

Let's consider David, a mid-level manager who struggled with speaking up in leadership meetings. Every time he had an idea, he second-guessed himself, thinking, *What if I'm wrong? What if I sound incompetent?* As a result, he often stayed quiet, missed opportunities, and watched others lead while he remained in the background.

After learning about power posing and positive self-talk, David made a small but powerful change. Before every meeting, he stood tall in a private office, practiced a power pose for two minutes, and told himself: *"My ideas matter. I am here for a reason."*

At his next meeting, David raised his hand and shared an idea with confidence. To his surprise, his colleagues respected his input, engaged in discussion, and implemented his suggestions. Over time, this became a habit, and his leadership presence grew exponentially; not because he suddenly became smarter, but because he finally believed in himself.

Confidence Is a Decision, Not Just a Feeling

Confidence isn't something you wait for; it's something you choose every day. Great leaders don't always feel confident, but they act with confidence despite uncertainty. By practicing confidence-building habits daily, you can train your brain to operate from a place of assurance rather than hesitation.

Final Principle: Courage Creates Confidence

Many people believe that confidence comes first; that once they *feel* confident, they'll take action. But the truth is, action comes first, and confidence follows.

Great leaders don't wait until they feel 100% ready before stepping into leadership moments. They take action despite fear, despite doubt, and despite uncertainty. Over time, each small act of courage builds momentum, experience, and belief in their own abilities.

Think about these situations:

- The first time you spoke up in a meeting, it felt uncomfortable.

- The first time you took on a leadership role, you doubted yourself.

- The first time you made a tough decision, you feared you might fail.

But you did it anyway, and with each step, your confidence grew.

Confidence is not the absence of fear. It is the decision to act in spite of fear. [28] That's what separates leaders from followers.

Action Steps For Today:

1. **Power Pose Before a Challenge:** Stand tall and hold a confident posture before your next big leadership moment.

2. **Reframe Negative Thoughts:** When self-doubt creeps in, replace it with a leadership affirmation.

3. **Act Confident, Even If You Don't Feel It Yet:** Confidence follows action. Show up with conviction, and belief will follow.

4. **Whenever you feel hesitation, doubt, or fear creeping in, ask yourself:** *"If I were already a confident leader, what action would I take right now?"* Then, do that.

THE LEADERSHIP CHALLENGE IS ABOUT TAKING ACTION-SO STEP UP, OWN YOUR LEADERSHIP PRESENCE, AND WATCH YOUR IMPACT GROW.

Day 6: The Art of Decision-Making

The Art of Thinking Clearly Under Pressure

"In any moment of decision, the best thing you can do is the right thing, the next best thing is the wrong thing, and the worst thing you can do is nothing." - Theodore Roosevelt [29]

Leadership isn't about having all the answers; it's about making decisive, well-informed choices even when uncertainty creeps in. Some leaders get paralyzed by overthinking, fearing the wrong choice will cost them credibility, time, or resources. Others make rash, emotion-driven decisions without considering long-term consequences. The best leaders find a balance; they make confident, strategic decisions that move things forward.

The Hidden Cost of Indecision

Meet Alex, a rising executive known for his deep analytical skills. His boss admires his ability to spot risks, and his team trusts him to think through problems carefully. But there is one problem: Alex struggles to pull the trigger on tough decisions. When a major opportunity arises for his company to expand, Alex spends weeks gathering data, debating with colleagues, and weighing every possible outcome. By the time he finally makes a decision, the opportunity has passed, and the competition has already taken action.

In contrast, his colleague Rachel, though equally analytical, has a structured approach to making decisions quickly and effectively. She gathers key information, assesses risks, and makes calls without unnecessary delays. Her decisions aren't always perfect, but they keep her team moving forward.

This story highlights a critical truth: Indecision is more damaging than making the wrong decision. While bad decisions can be corrected, hesitation leads to missed opportunities and stagnation.

The Three Pillars of Strong Decision-Making

1. The 70% Rule: Deciding When You Have Enough Information

Amazon's Jeff Bezos follows what he calls the **"70% Rule"** for decision-making. He says, *"Most decisions should be made with about 70% of the information you wish you had."* [30]

If you wait until you have 100% certainty, you're already too late. Top leaders recognize that:

- Gathering data is important, but endless analysis leads to paralysis.

- You will never have all the answers, so focus on making the best choice with what you know now.

- The key is speed and adaptability. If the decision turns out to be wrong, adjust quickly.

The next time you're stuck on a decision, ask yourself:

- *Do I have at least 70% of the necessary information?*

- *If so, what's the worst that could happen if I move forward?*

2.The OODA Loop: A Framework for Fast, Effective Decisions

There may be times when you don't even have 70% of the information to make a decision. If this occurs, try this strategy. It was originally developed by military strategist John Boyd. The OODA Loop is a powerful framework for rapid, adaptive decision-making in uncertain and high-stakes situations. Leaders who use this method can make better, faster decisions by continuously assessing their environment and adjusting their approach.

How It Works:

1. **Observe** – Gather relevant information and assess the current situation.

2. **Orient** – Analyze the data, recognize patterns, and consider different perspectives.

3. **Decide** – Choose the best course of action based on the information available.

4. **Act** – Implement the decision while staying flexible and ready to adapt.

The OODA Loop helps leaders navigate complex and fast-changing situations by emphasizing speed, adaptability, and continuous learning. It's especially useful in uncertain environments, crisis management, and competitive industries where decisions must be made quickly. [31]

By practicing this approach, you'll become a **faster, more confident decision-maker**.

The next time you need to make a rapid decision, try the **OODA Loop** based on the information you DO have. There are many times in leadership when we must make quick decisions with limited information.

3. The 10-10-10 Rule: Seeing Beyond the Immediate Impact

When faced with a tough decision, many leaders struggle because they focus too much on short-term emotions rather than long-term impact.

Best-selling author Suzy Welch developed the 10-10-10 Rule to help leaders make choices with clarity and confidence. [32]

It works like this:

- How will I feel about this decision in 10 minutes? (Immediate reaction)

- How will I feel about it in 10 months? (Mid-term consequences)

- How will I feel about it in 10 years? (Long-term impact)

For example, imagine you're debating whether to fire a struggling employee.

- Here iln 10 minutes, it might feel uncomfortable.

- In 10 months, the team may be functioning better because you hired someone stronger.

- In 10 years, you'll look back and realize it was the right choice for everyone involved.

The next time you're stuck on a tough decision, apply the **10-10-10 Rule** to gain perspective and avoid knee-jerk reactions.

Case Study: How Jeff Bezos Uses "The Two Types of Decisions" Rule

Amazon's Jeff Bezos follows a simple decision-making principle:

- Type 1 Decisions: Big, irreversible choices. These require deep analysis and caution (e.g., entering a new market).

- Type 2 Decisions: Reversible, lower-risk choices. These should be made quickly (e.g., testing a new feature).

For example, when Amazon decided whether to launch Prime, it was a Type 1 decision, high risk, major investment. They conducted extensive research. But when testing same-day delivery, it was a Type 2 decision, easily reversible. They rolled it out quickly and adjusted it based on feedback.[33]

Leadership Lesson: Not all decisions require months of debate. If a decision is reversible, don't overthink it-act.

Exercise: Sharpen Your Decision-Making Skills This Week

Step 1: Identify a decision you've been avoiding

- Write it down, then think about why you have been putting it off.

Step 2: Apply one of today's frameworks

- Use the 70% Rule to see if you have enough info.

- Use the OODA Loop for a rapid, adaptive decision-making process.

- Use the 10-10-10 Rule to look at long-term impact.

Step 3: Make the decision, and move forward

- Once you've analyzed it, **commit and take action.**

Final Principle: Leaders Decide-And Then Adapt

"Deciding what not to do is as important as deciding what to do."
-Steve Jobs[34]

The best leaders make decisions with conviction and clarity and then adapt as needed. At the end of the day, great leaders don't wait for the perfect answer; they take action and then adjust.

- Average leaders hesitate.

- Great leaders make decisions and refine them as they go.

Your Action Steps for Today:

- Make **one decision** you've been avoiding.

- Use a **decision-making framework** to support your choice.

- **Move forward** with confidence and adaptability.

ARE YOU READY TO STEP INTO DECISION-MAKING MASTERY?

Day 7: Leading Through Setbacks

How Resilient Leaders Overcome Challenges and Inspire Others

Today, we'll explore why resilience is the #1 predictor of leadership success, how to build a resilient mindset, and practical strategies to bounce back stronger from setbacks.

Picture this: A promising new initiative flops. A critical hire quits unexpectedly. A high-stakes project derails at the last moment.

As a leader, failure isn't just possible-it's inevitable.

What separates great leaders from the rest isn't avoiding setbacks; it's how they respond. Some let failures define them, becoming discouraged and hesitant. Others see failures as refining them; learning, adapting, and growing stronger. What kind of leader will you be?

"Do not judge me by my successes; judge me by how many times I fell down and got back up again." -Nelson Mandela[35]

Why Resilience Is a Non-Negotiable Leadership Skill

Resilience isn't just about surviving tough times; it's about leading others through them.

Research shows:

- **90% of top-performing leaders** exhibit high resilience. *(Harvard Business Review)* [36]

- **Companies with resilient leadership** recover 2x faster from crises. *(McKinsey & Company)* [37]

- **Employees are 68% more engaged** when their leader demonstrates resilience. *(Gallup)* [38]

Resilient leaders create a culture where failure isn't feared; instead, they use it as fuel for growth. But how do you build resilience when challenges hit hard? Try out the framework below.

The 3-Step Resilience Framework[39]

Step 1: Reframe the Setback *(Control the Narrative)*

When failure strikes, your first reaction matters most.

Unproductive Leaders Say:

- *"I'm not cut out for this."*

- *"I'll never recover."*

- *"Everything is ruined."*

Resilient Leaders Say:

- *"What can I learn from this?"*

- *"How do I turn this into a stepping stone?"*

- *"What's the next right move?"*

For example, when Oprah was fired from her first TV job, she could've given up. Instead, she reframed it, seeing it as proof that she needed to create her own path. That mindset shift led her to become one of the most influential television figures of all time.

Your Turn: Think of a recent setback. How can you reframe it as a learning opportunity instead of a failure?

Step 2: Regroup and Strategize (*Bounce, Don't Break*)

After a setback, pause, but don't stop.

Ask yourself:

- *What worked?*

- *What didn't work?*

- *What will I do differently next time?*

For example, when Walt Disney was told he "lacked creativity" and was fired from a newspaper job, [40] he could have let that define him. Instead, he kept pursuing his vision, overcoming multiple business failures before finally creating Disney Studios. His resilience built an entertainment empire that continues to inspire the world. The lesson? Failure isn't a stop sign; it's a course correction.

Your Turn: Write down one adjustment you can make based on a past failure.

Step 3: Lead with Transparency (*Turn Setbacks into Stories*)

The best leaders don't hide failures; they share them.

Why?

- It builds trust. People respect leaders who admit challenges.

- It sets the tone. If you normalize learning from setbacks, your team will too.

- It inspires resilience in others.

For example, Howard Schultz, Starbucks' CEO, openly shares how he failed multiple times before building a global brand. Instead of hiding his mistakes, he used them to teach and empower others.[41]

Your Turn: The next time you face a setback, be open about it and frame it as a learning opportunity for your team.

Case Study: How Sara Blakely Built Spanx on Rejection

Sara Blakely, founder of Spanx, didn't just face one failure; she faced hundreds.[42]

- She was rejected by multiple manufacturers.

- Investors laughed at her idea.

- She had zero experience in business or fashion.

But she kept going. Why? Because of a simple lesson her dad taught her growing up. Every night at dinner, he'd ask, *"What did you fail at today?"* Instead of seeing failure as bad, she learned to see it as a sign of growth. That mindset shift fueled her resilience, and today, Spanx is a billion-dollar brand.

Leadership Lesson: If you never fail, you're not pushing yourself hard enough.

Exercise: Build Your Resilience Muscle

Step 1: Identify a Past Setback

Think of a leadership challenge that didn't go as planned.

- *What happened?*

- *How did you react?*

- *What lesson did it teach you?*

Step 2: Apply the Resilience Framework

- Reframe it. *What's the lesson, not the loss?*

- Regroup. *What's one strategic change you'd make next time?*

- Lead with transparency. *How can you share this story to inspire others?*

The more you do this, the stronger your resilience will become.

The Research: Why Setbacks Strengthen Leaders

- **Angela Duckworth's research on "grit"** found that **persistence beats talent** in long-term success. *(University of Pennsylvania)* [43]

- **Organizations that embrace failure innovate 5x faster** than those that punish it. *(MIT Sloan Management Review)* [44]

- **Employees trust leaders more** when they admit challenges but keep moving forward. *(Gallup)* [45]

"It is impossible to live without failing at something, unless you live so cautiously that you might as well not have lived at all." -J.K. Rowling[46]

Final Principle: Your Response Defines Your Leadership

At its core, resilience isn't about avoiding setbacks; it's about mastering your response to them.

- Weak leaders get stuck in failure.

- Strong leaders look for the lesson to be learned and move forward.

Your Action Steps for Today:

- Think of a recent failure and **reframe it into a lesson.**

- Apply the **3-Step Resilience Framework** to a challenge you're facing.

- Commit to leading **with transparency, learning, and persistence.**

ARE YOU READY TO LEAD THROUGH SETBACKS LIKE A PRO?

DAY 8: THE ART OF TIME MANAGEMENT

WHY TIME MANAGEMENT = LEADERSHIP EFFECTIVENESS

Leadership is not just about vision, decision-making, and influence; it's about execution. The best leaders maximize their time by ensuring they are focused on the right tasks and avoiding distractions that drain productivity.

"The difference between successful people and really successful people is that really successful people say 'no' to almost everything."
-Warren Buffett [47]

Think about that for a moment. **Leadership is about prioritization.** The leaders who make the greatest impact don't just work harder; they work smarter by mastering their time.

The Leadership-Time Paradox

One of the greatest ironies of leadership is that the more responsibility you take on, the less time you seem to have. Yet, the best leaders operate under the same 24-hour constraint as everyone else. So, what separates highly effective leaders from overwhelmed ones?

- They **protect their time fiercely** and focus on high-impact activities.

- They **delegate and automate** anything that doesn't require their direct input.

- They **schedule priorities** rather than just reacting to endless demands.

This isn't about working longer hours; it's about taking ownership of your time.

Case Study: How Bill Gates Structures His Time for Maximum Productivity

When it comes to effective time management, few leaders have been as disciplined and strategic as Bill Gates. As the co-founder of Microsoft and a global philanthropist, Gates has had to juggle multiple high-impact projects while ensuring he stays focused on the most critical work.

How Bill Gates Manages His Time Effectively

1. The "Think Week" Strategy-Dedicated Time for Deep Focus

One of Gates' most famous time-management strategies is his "Think Week." Twice a year, he completely isolates himself in a cabin, cutting off all distractions, including emails and meetings. He spends this time reading, reflecting, and thinking deeply about the future of technology, business, and philanthropy.

"I had to take control of my time to focus on the things that would have the biggest impact." – Bill Gates[48]

This practice has led to some of his biggest breakthroughs, including early investments in internet technology and global health initiatives.

2. He Schedules Every Minute-But Leaves Room for Flexibility

Like many high-performing leaders, Gates structures his day into blocks of time, ensuring every moment is spent productively. However, unlike rigid micro-scheduling, he leaves flexibility for unexpected priorities and ensures time for learning, which he believes is a key to long-term success.

3. He Prioritizes Learning and Thinking Over Busyness

Gates is an avid reader, consuming about 50 books per year, and he dedicates daily time to learning. He believes that leaders should spend more time thinking, not just doing, as it leads to better decision-making and innovation. [49]

The key takeaway from Gates' approach? Time is your most valuable asset-treat it with the same level of strategy as your biggest business decision. In the end, it is not about getting more done; it is about getting the right things done.

The Eisenhower Matrix: Prioritization Like a President

Dwight D. Eisenhower, the 34th President of the United States and a former five-star general, was known for his ability to make decisions under intense pressure. Inspired by his approach to time management, leadership expert Stephen Covey later popularized a simple yet powerful prioritization framework-now known as the Eisenhower Matrix- which helps individuals distinguish between what is urgent and what is truly important.[50]

This tool categorizes tasks into four quadrants:

Exercise: Apply the Eisenhower Matrix Today

List out everything on your plate, from major leadership initiatives to minor emails. Then, categorize each task using the Eisenhower Matrix:

1. What must be done immediately? (DO IT)

2. What should be scheduled for later? (SCHEDULE IT)

3. What should be delegated? (DELEGATE IT)

4. What should be cut completely? (ELIMINATE IT)

This forces clarity and ensures you're leading with focus instead of drowning in distractions.

The Biggest Leadership Time Traps (and How to Avoid Them)

Even the best leaders fall into common time-wasting traps. Here's how to recognize and fix them:

1. The "Always Available" Trap

- The Problem: Leaders often feel obligated to be accessible 24/7, answering emails, attending every meeting, and responding instantly.

- The Fix: Batch-check emails and messages at set times. Block out "deep work" periods where you're unavailable. (Depending on your field, I understand this is not always an option.)

2. The "Meeting Overload" Trap

- The Problem: Meetings consume massive amounts of time, often without clear objectives.

- The Fix: Cancel unnecessary meetings. Require a clear agenda for every meeting. If it can be handled via email, skip the meeting. (Unless, it's a meeting with your boss!)

3. The "Fake Productivity" Trap

- The Problem: Mistaking busyness for progress. Just because your day is packed doesn't mean it was productive.

- The Fix: Start every day by identifying your top 3 priorities and ensure those get done first.

Real-Life Leadership Story: The "$10,000 Per Hour" Mindset

A mentor once asked a young leader: "Are you doing $10 tasks, $100 tasks, or $10,000 tasks?" [51]

This question shifted everything for the young leader. Instead of spending hours on small tasks, he started delegating anything that wasn't a high-value leadership activity. Within a year, his influence and productivity skyrocketed.

Ask yourself: "Am I spending time on tasks that move my leadership forward, or am I trapped in busy work?"

Want to level up your time management as a leader?

Start with these three simple steps:

1. Start Every Day with Intent

- Instead of checking emails first thing, write down your top 3 priorities for the day.

- Ask: *"What is the most valuable thing I can do today?"*

- Focus on high-impact work before responding to external demands.

2. Set Boundaries Around Your Time

- Block uninterrupted deep work sessions on your calendar.

- Schedule "no meeting" hours where you focus only on leadership priorities.

- Train your team to solve problems independently instead of always needing your input.

3. Use the "Two-Minute Rule" [52]

- If something takes less than 2 minutes, do it immediately.

- If it takes longer than 2 minutes, schedule it, delegate it, or eliminate it.

Final Principle: Control Time, Control Your Leadership

Time is the ultimate leadership currency, and how you spend it determines your impact, influence, and success. The most effective leaders aren't those who work the most hours—they're the ones who master their time.

"Your time is limited, so don't waste it living someone else's life."-Steve Jobs[53]

Leadership is about making time for what truly matters. Every minute spent on the wrong thing is a minute lost from building your vision.

Your Action Steps For Today:

- Look at your schedule. Are you in control of your time, or is your time controlling you?

- Identify one major shift you can make to take back your time and lead more effectively.

THE BEST LEADERS DON'T LET BUSYNESS STEAL THEIR GREATNESS.
MAKE THE SHIFT TODAY.

Day 9: Leading with Integrity and Authenticity

Why Trust Is a Leader's Most Valuable Currency

In leadership, **trust isn't just important; it's everything.** You can have the best strategies, the most innovative ideas, and a brilliant vision, but if people don't trust you, none of it matters.

"It takes 20 years to build a reputation and five minutes to ruin it."
-Warren Buffett [54]

Leaders who prioritize integrity and authenticity create teams that are loyal, engaged, and willing to go the extra mile. Without it, people disengage, morale crumbles, and leadership influence disappears.

In today's world, where employees, customers, and stakeholders crave honest, ethical leadership, authenticity isn't just a nice-to-have; it's a must-have. But what does leading with integrity and authenticity really mean? And how do you cultivate it in your leadership?

Integrity vs. Authenticity: What's the Difference?

These two words are often used interchangeably, but they are distinct qualities that work together:

- **Integrity** is about doing the right thing-even when no one is watching.

- **Authenticity** is about being real, transparent, and true to your values.

The most trusted leaders embody both. They are consistent, honest, and aligned with their principles.

The Impact of Leading with Integrity and Authenticity

When leaders prioritize integrity and authenticity:

- Teams trust them more-Trust leads to loyalty and engagement.

- Decisions are respected-Even hard choices are accepted when people believe in your honesty.

- A strong culture is built-Transparency and honesty create an open, ethical work environment.

- Long-term success follows-Integrity builds lasting relationships and sustainable leadership.

In contrast, when integrity is compromised, even in small ways, it leads to:

- Distrust and disengagement-People will question motives and resist leadership.

- High turnover-Employees won't stay in an environment lacking honesty.

- Reputation damage-Once lost, trust is difficult (sometimes impossible) to regain.[55]

Case Study: Howard Schultz and Authentic Leadership at Starbucks

Few leaders have demonstrated integrity and authenticity in business better than Howard Schultz, the former CEO of Starbucks. When Schultz took over Starbucks, he didn't just focus on profits; he built a company that prioritized people first. His leadership was rooted in honesty, responsibility, and care.

Examples of Schultz's commitment to authentic leadership:

- He was one of the first CEOs to offer healthcare benefits to both full-time and part-time employees, long before it was common practice.

- During the 2008 financial crisis, Starbucks faced major losses. Instead of making quiet, behind-the-scenes cuts, Schultz held town hall meetings to openly share financial challenges with employees.

- He shut down all 7,100 Starbucks stores for an entire day to retrain baristas, prioritizing quality over short-term profits.

This approach wasn't always popular or easy, but it built an unshakable level of trust with employees, customers, and stakeholders. [56]

Be transparent, stay true to your values, and don't compromise integrity-even when it's difficult.[4]

Practical Example: The Manager Who Admitted a Mistake

A few years ago, a department head at a growing tech startup made a costly mistake, one that led to a major client pulling out of a deal.

Instead of hiding the mistake or blaming the team, she called an all-hands meeting and said: *"I take full responsibility. I misjudged the risks, and we lost an opportunity because of it. Here's what I learned, and here's how we prevent this from happening again."*

Her team respected her even more after that moment. Why? Because she showed integrity by taking responsibility, she was authentic by openly discussing failure and turned it into a learning moment rather than a blame game.

- The result? Her team became more willing to take ownership, and trust in her leadership grew stronger.

- Lesson learned? Leaders don't have to be perfect; they just have to be honest, accountable, and transparent.

Steps to Strengthen Integrity and Authenticity

1. Model What You Expect

"The standard you walk past is the standard you accept." -David Hurley[58]

- If you want honesty, be honest-even when it's uncomfortable.

- If you want accountability, take responsibility first.

- If you want transparency, openly share insights with your team.

2. Keep Your Promises (Even the Small Ones)

- Integrity is built through consistent follow-through.

- If you say you'll respond to an email, respond.

- If you commit to a deadline, meet it-or communicate why you can't.

3. Admit When You're Wrong

- People trust leaders who own their mistakes.

- Say, *"I got that wrong. Here's what I'll do differently next time."*

- Vulnerability creates authenticity and credibility.

4. Communicate the 'Why' Behind Decisions

- Employees resist change when they don't understand the reasoning.

- Instead of just making decisions, explain why.

- Transparency builds trust in leadership direction.

Exercise: Identify One Area to Improve Transparency & Honesty

Reflect on your leadership today:

1. Where are you not being fully transparent?

   - Are you holding back difficult but necessary conversations?

   - Are you sugarcoating feedback instead of giving direct, honest insights?

- Are you making decisions without properly communicating the "why" to your team?

2. Where can you improve integrity?

  - Have you ever cut corners on ethics because it seemed harmless?

  - Have you ever promised something you couldn't deliver?

  - Have you ever failed to follow through on a commitment?

Final Principle: Integrity Creates Legacy

At the end of the day, leadership is about more than short-term success. It's about the legacy you leave behind.

When you lead with integrity and authenticity:

- Your words carry weight.

- Your decisions inspire confidence.

- Your leadership outlasts you.

> **Action Step For Today:**
> Choose one area where you can be more honest, transparent, or accountable, and commit to improving it this week.

TRUST IS EARNED DAILY, AND THE STRONGEST LEADERS NEVER STOP EARNING IT.

DAY 10: DAILY REFLECTION AND LEADERSHIP JOURNALING

SELF-REFLECTION AS A LEADERSHIP SUPERPOWER

The most effective leaders don't just move forward blindly; they take intentional pauses to assess their progress, refine their approach, and learn from their experiences.[59] Yet, in today's fast-paced world, reflection often takes a backseat to urgent tasks, emails, and meetings. Many leaders believe they don't have time to sit and reflect, but in reality, not taking the time costs them more in the long run.

When leaders don't reflect, they:

- Repeat the same mistakes.

- Overreact to situations and respond without fully thinking things through.

- Lose sight of their values and leadership purpose.

- Fail to recognize patterns in their decision-making.

On the other hand, when leaders pause and reflect, they:

- Make wiser and more informed decisions.

- Align their actions with their values and mission.

- Become proactive rather than reactive leaders.

Daily journaling is one of the simplest yet most powerful ways to develop self-awareness and become a better leader. I'll be honest. I know I need to do better at journaling, but I have yet to find a system that will work for me in the long term. For me, the best time to reflect is right when I get home. It gives me the time to decompress from the day a bit. I can then refocus my attention on my family.

Why Reflection Transforms Leadership

John Dewey, a pioneer in education and learning, said:

> *"We do not learn from experience... we learn from reflecting on experience."* [60]

Without reflection, even the best experiences are wasted. Many people assume that simply doing something over and over makes them better at it.

Experience alone doesn't drive growth-reflecting on it does.

Think about two leaders:

- Susie has been in leadership for 10 years but never takes time to reflect. She reacts the same way to problems repeatedly, repeats the same mistakes, and has difficulty seeing how her leadership impacts others.

- Kathy also has 10 years of experience but takes 5-10 minutes daily to reflect. She identifies patterns, adjusts her leadership style, and, as a result, grows into a more self-aware, effective leader.

This is why some leaders with fewer years of experience surpass those with decades of leadership; they make reflection a habit. Even top CEOs, world-class athletes, and successful entrepreneurs set aside time to reflect on their performance and refine their approach.

Case Study: How Journaling Shaped Marcus Aurelius's Leadership

Marcus Aurelius, the Roman Emperor from 161 to 180 AD, is remembered as one of history's wisest and most reflective leaders. His personal journal, later published as *Meditations*, is a collection of deep reflections on leadership, character, and self-improvement.[61]

What made his journaling powerful?

1. He used it for self-discipline.

   - Every day, he reminded himself to stay humble, patient, and wise.

   - He wrote about controlling his emotions and not letting power corrupt him.

2. He reflected on challenges.

   - Instead of complaining about difficulties, he wrote about how to approach them rationally.

   - He saw obstacles as opportunities for growth.

3. He reinforced his values.

   - He constantly reminded himself to act with honor, integrity, and justice.

His journal was his personal leadership guide that helped him stay grounded, disciplined, and reflective.

Here's what we can learn:

- Reflection helps you stay intentional instead of just reacting.

- Writing your thoughts makes you a more self-aware, thoughtful leader.

- You don't need to be a philosopher or emperor-just 5 minutes of journaling can transform your leadership.

Practical Example: The CEO Who Saved His Company Through Reflection

The CEO of a growing restaurant chain was struggling. His team was burned out, employees felt disconnected, and profits were slipping. Instead of making impulsive decisions, he started daily journaling:

- He wrote about what was going wrong.

- He analyzed his own leadership mistakes.

- He identified blind spots in communication and culture.

Through this reflection, he realized:

1. He wasn't listening enough.

2. His team was overwhelmed with too many projects.

3. He needed to simplify goals and focus on clarity.

Over the next months, he adjusted his leadership approach based on his reflections. The result? Employee engagement skyrocketed, the company turned profitable again, and he became a more thoughtful, effective leader. Reflection wasn't just a nice habit for him to develop; it was the key to solving real leadership challenges.

Exercise: Build the Habit of Reflecting

1. Set a Consistent Time [62]

- Morning Reflection: Set intentions for the day ahead.

- Evening Reflection: Analyze what you learned and how you grew.

2. Keep It Simple [63]

- Don't aim for pages of writing-start with just 3-5 bullet points.

- You can even use voice notes if your writing feels slow.

3. Be Honest with Yourself [64]

- Reflection is only valuable if you're genuine.

- It's not about looking good on paper-it's about growth.

4. Review Past Entries [65]

- Go back and read previous reflections.

- Look for patterns-what keeps showing up? What lessons are repeating?

Final Principle: Growth Requires Reflection

If you go through life without reflection, you repeat the same mistakes. But when you pause, reflect, and learn, you become stronger, wiser, and more intentional. The best leaders never stop learning—and journaling is the shortcut to lifelong leadership growth.

Your Action Steps For Today: Start a Leadership Reflection Journal

Now it's your turn. Starting today, take 5-10 minutes at the end of your day to reflect.
Journaling Prompts to Try:

1. What went well today? Celebrate successes, no matter how small.

2. What could I have done better? Identify one leadership improvement area.

3. How did I communicate with my team today? Was I clear, supportive, and approachable?

4. Did I act according to my values? Integrity, authenticity, and honesty-did I uphold them?

5. What is one leadership lesson from today? Every day provides a learning moment.

Try This: Commit to one week of reflection and see how it changes your leadership.

"Experience alone doesn't make you better-evaluated experience does." -John C. Maxwell[66]

PART 2

DAYS 11-20: LEADING OTHERS

DAY 11: THE POWER OF ACTIVE LISTENING

WHY THE BEST LEADERS LISTEN MORE THAN THEY TALK

Imagine sitting in a conversation with someone who constantly interrupts, rushes to give advice, or seems more focused on what they'll say next rather than what you're saying.

Now, think about the opposite: someone who listens intently, makes you feel truly heard, and responds thoughtfully. Which person would you rather follow as a leader?

Leadership isn't just about making big decisions or giving inspiring speeches. One of the most underrated but powerful leadership skills is listening. Many people assume that great leaders are the ones who speak confidently, deliver compelling messages, or command attention in a room. Craig Groeschel said, "*The best leaders listen more than they talk,*" [67] and that's what makes them influential.

Why Does Listening Matter in Leadership?

As a leader, your success depends on your ability to:

- Understand your team's needs, challenges, and ideas.

- Build trust and relationships.

- Make informed, strategic decisions.

- Create a culture where people feel heard and valued.

Without **active listening**, leaders risk making poor decisions, losing engagement from their teams, and creating environments where innovation and trust suffer.[68]

"When people talk, listen completely. Most people never listen."
-Ernest Hemingway [69]

Listening isn't just about hearing words; it's about understanding and connecting. Your goal should be to **listen to understand, not just to respond**. When you truly listen, you create an environment where people feel valued and heard, which is essential for strong leadership.

"Most people do not listen with the intent to understand; they listen with the intent to reply."-Stephen Covey[70]

Case Study: How Oprah Winfrey Uses Listening to Build Deep Connections

Oprah Winfrey has built her empire on one core skill: **active listening.** From interviewing world leaders to everyday people, Oprah has an uncanny ability to make people feel seen and heard. How does she do it?

She Listens Without Interrupting.

- She gives people space to fully express themselves before responding.

- This makes her interviews feel deep, thoughtful, and meaningful.

She Uses the "Tell Me More" Approach.

Instead of jumping to the next question, she digs deeper by asking,

- *"Can you tell me more about that?"*

- *"What was that experience like for you?"*

This shows she is genuinely interested in the other person's thoughts.

She Listens for Emotion, Not Just Words.

- She picks up on tone, facial expressions, and pauses, which helps her respond with empathy and authenticity.

Because of her active listening, Oprah has built **trust, influence, and connection** with millions.

If you want to inspire and lead others, learn to be a better listener. When you listen well, people not only open up, but they trust you to lead them.

Exercise: The 3-Second Pause Technique: How to Instantly Become a Better Listener

One of the simplest yet most powerful ways to improve your listening skills is to use the 3-Second Pause Technique.[71]

Step 1: When Someone Finishes Speaking, Pause for 3 Seconds

- Don't jump in immediately with your response.

- Take a breath and let the words sink in.

Step 2: Use This Time to Process What Was Said

Ask yourself:

- *Did I truly understand what they meant?*

- *What emotions are they expressing?*

- *What question can I ask to clarify or go deeper?*

Step 3: Respond Thoughtfully

Instead of rushing to give advice, ask:

- *"That's really interesting. Can you elaborate on that?"*

- *"It sounds like this is really important to you. Can you tell me more?"*

This simple habit does two powerful things:

1. It prevents you from interrupting or thinking about your response instead of listening.

2. It makes the speaker feel genuinely heard and respected.

"Silence isn't empty. It's full of answers." -Unknown[72]

Practical Example: The Manager Who Transformed Team Morale

A department manager, Brittany, was struggling with a disengaged team. Employees felt unheard, and team meetings were one-sided, and Brittany did all the talking. Morale was at an all-time low. After attending a leadership seminar, she committed to listening more intentionally.

Here's what she changed:

- She started using the 3-Second Pause, which made people feel she was actually absorbing their words.

- She asked follow-up questions instead of moving on too quickly.

- She stopped jumping to conclusions and gave space for team members to express themselves fully.

The result?

- Employees opened up more and shared better ideas.

- Team morale improved significantly.

- Productivity and engagement improved.

It wasn't a major strategy shift; it was simply the power of listening to understand, not just to respond. Listening is the most powerful tool a leader has—use it wisely.

Final Principle: Influence Begins with Listening

Great leaders aren't the ones who **speak the most;** they're the ones who **listen the best.** When people feel heard, they:

- Trust you more.

- Follow your leadership more willingly.

- Feel valued and motivated.

Action Steps For Today:

1. Start Every Conversation with the Intent to Listen
- Remind yourself: *"My goal is to understand, not just reply."*

2. Use the 3-Second Pause
- Let silence work in your favor and show you're fully processing what was said.

3. Ask Clarifying Questions-Instead of responding immediately, try:
- *"Can you tell me more about that?"*

- *"What's the biggest challenge you're facing with this?"*

4. Eliminate Distractions
- Put your phone away and close your laptop.

- Give the speaker your full attention.

"THE MOST IMPORTANT THING IN COMMUNICATION IS HEARING WHAT ISN'T SAID." -PETER DRUCKER [73]

Day 12: Giving and Receiving Feedback Like a Leader

Why Feedback is the Secret to Leadership Growth

Imagine you've been putting your heart and soul into a project for months. You finally get the chance to present your work so far to your boss; you're hoping for feedback that will help you improve or let you know if you are heading in the right direction. Instead, you hear: *"This isn't what I expected; you're way off."* You get no details, no direction, and no encouragement.

Now, imagine the same scenario but with this response from your boss: *"I appreciate the effort you put into this. Let's look at a few areas where we can make it even stronger. When you presented the data, I noticed some key points were missing, which made it hard to follow. If we add those in, it will create a clearer picture for our stakeholders. What do you think?"*

This is the same message with two completely different impacts. **Feedback can make or break motivation, confidence, and performance.** Yet, so many leaders struggle to deliver it in a way that inspires improvement instead of causing frustration.

Great leaders not only give effective feedback but also know how to receive feedback.They seek it out, embrace it, and use it as a tool for growth rather than a personal attack.

"We all need people who will give us feedback. That's how we improve." – Bill Gates[74]

Whether you're leading a team, mentoring someone, or working to improve yourself, learning how to give and receive feedback effectively is one of the most valuable leadership skills you can develop.

Before we talk about how to deliver feedback well, let's clarify the difference between criticism and constructive feedback.

- **Criticism** focuses on the person and often feels like an attack. It's vague, negative, and demotivating. For example: *"You're not a good presenter. You need to do better."*

- **Constructive feedback** focuses on specific behaviors and how they impact the situation. It offers ideas and suggestions instead of just pointing out mistakes. For example: *"Your presentation had great content, but I noticed you were reading from your slides instead of engaging with the audience. Let's work on making it more dynamic next time."*[75]

Great leaders deliver feedback that builds people up, not tears them down.

Now, let's look at how to deliver powerful, growth-focused feedback using the SBI Model. The **SBI Model** (Situation-Behavior-Impact) is a structured way to deliver feedback that is clear, actionable, and non-threatening. [76]

How It Works

1. **Situation** – Describe the specific moment when the behavior occurred.

2. **Behavior** – Focus on what the person did (not who they are).

3. **Impact** – Explain the effect of their behavior on the team, project, or goal.

Example of SBI in Action

Instead of saying: *"You were really rude in the meeting."*

Use the SBI Model: *"During the meeting yesterday morning (Situation), I noticed you interrupted Sarah multiple times while she was explaining her idea (Behavior). That made it difficult for her to share her thoughts, and I could see she felt frustrated (Impact). Let's work on creating space for everyone to contribute."*

Practice SBI:

1. Identify one piece of feedback you need to give.

2. Use the SBI format to frame it in a constructive way. (write it out)

3. Deliver it with a focus on improvement, not blame.

Case Study: How Netflix Builds a Culture of Radical Feedback

One of the most admired leadership cultures in the world belongs to Netflix. At the heart of its success is a principle called **Radical Candor,**[77] a feedback culture where honesty is valued over comfort.

How Netflix Does Feedback Differently:[78]

1. **Feedback is expected, not avoided:** At Netflix, employees at all levels are encouraged to give and receive candid feedback constantly, not just during formal reviews.

2. **No sugarcoating, but always with care:** Employees are trained to give direct feedback, but in a way that is helpful, not hurtful.

3. **Leaders lead by example:** Netflix executives openly seek feedback from their teams, proving that growth is more important than ego.

"The best feedback isn't about making people comfortable; it's about making them better." – Patty McCord, Former Netflix Chief Talent Officer [79]

Exercise: Create Your Own Feedback Culture

- **Encourage feedback**: Start meetings by inviting open input.

- **Make feedback a habit**: Don't wait for annual reviews; give real-time coaching.

- **Model it yourself:** Ask your team, *"What's one thing I could do better as a leader?"*

A leader who actively seeks and gives feedback earns trust, respect, and long-term success.

How to Receive Feedback Like a Leader

Giving feedback is only one side of the coin. Great leaders also know how to accept it.

Three Mindset Shifts for Receiving Feedback Well

1. Assume positive intent – Feedback isn't an attack; it's an opportunity to grow.

2. Listen fully before responding – Resist the urge to explain or defend immediately.

3. Ask clarifying questions – *"Can you give me an example?"* or *"What would you suggest I do differently?"*

The One-Week Feedback Challenge

For the next 7 days, challenge yourself to:

- Give one piece of constructive feedback every day.

- Ask for feedback on something specific you're working on.

The more you practice, the stronger your leadership will become.

Final Principle: Feedback is a Gift

At the end of the day, feedback, whether giving or receiving, isn't about judgment. It's about growth. The leaders who thrive don't shy away from tough conversations. They embrace feedback as the key to continuous improvement.

Action Steps For Today:

- Give one piece of feedback today using the SBI model.

- Ask someone for feedback and receive it with an open mind.

EVERY GREAT LEADER IS A STUDENT FIRST. BE BOLD, BE COACHABLE, AND KEEP GROWING. COMMIT TO BEING A LEADER WHO GIVES FEEDBACK THAT EMPOWERS AND RECEIVES FEEDBACK THAT FUELS GROWTH.

DAY 13: COACHING VS. MANAGING

WHY GREAT LEADERS COACH, NOT JUST MANAGE

Think about the best leader you've ever worked with. Were they someone who simply assigned tasks, tracked deadlines, and checked off to-do lists? Or were they someone who challenged you to grow, encouraged your potential, and helped you become better than you thought possible?

The difference between a manager and a leader often comes down to this: Managers focus on tasks and processes, while leaders focus on people and potential.

"My job is not to be easy on people. My job is to make them better."
– Steve Jobs[80]

Coaching is what separates good leaders from truly transformational ones. It's not just about getting work done; it's about developing others to think, solve problems, and grow into leaders themselves. Coaching is the best approach to take if you want to build a high-performing team, increase engagement, and leave a lasting leadership impact.

The Difference Between Managing and Coaching

Before diving into how to coach effectively, let's break down the fundamental differences between managing and coaching[81]:

Managing	Coaching
• Focuses on tasks and execution • Directs and controls • Provides answers • Measures success by immediate results • Creates followers	• Focuses on growth and potential • Guides and empowers • Asks powerful questions • Measures success by long-term development • Develops future leaders

Many leaders start as managers, focused on efficiency, execution, and performance. But the most impactful leaders evolve into coaches, helping their teams learn, adapt, and grow beyond just completing tasks.

"Before you are a leader, success is all about growing yourself. When you become a leader, success is about growing others." –
Jack Welch [82]

So, how do you make the shift from managing to coaching? One of the best tools is the GROW Coaching Model.

Exercise: Apply the GROW Coaching Model in a Conversation

The **GROW Model** is one of the most effective coaching frameworks. It is used by top leaders and executive coaches worldwide. It provides a structured approach to helping people think critically, solve problems, and take ownership of their development.[83]

GROW Model Breakdown:

- **G – Goal** (What do you want to achieve?)

- **R – Reality** (Where are you now? What's happening?)

- **O – Options** (What could you do? What are possible solutions?)

- **W – Way Forward** (What will you do next?)

Example of GROW in Action

Imagine you're coaching a team member who is struggling with public speaking. Instead of saying: *"You need to work on your presentation skills."* Use the GROW model to guide them:[84]

- **Goal**: *"What's your ideal outcome when giving presentations?"*

- **Reality**: *"How do you currently feel about your presentations? What's working? What's challenging?"*

- **Options**: *"What are some things you could do to improve?"*

- **Way Forward**: *"What's one step you'll commit to before your next presentation?"*

This approach shifts ownership to them, which leads to greater accountability, confidence, and long-term growth.

Try the GROW Model Today

Find someone on your team who could benefit from coaching. Instead of giving advice, ask powerful questions using the GROW Model. Watch how it transforms the conversation!

Case Study: Bill Campbell -The Trillion-Dollar Coach

When it comes to leadership coaching, few people have had a greater impact than Bill Campbell. Campbell was known as the "Trillion-Dollar Coach" because of his behind-the-scenes role in coaching the world's top tech leaders, including:

✔ Steve Jobs (Apple)

✔ Larry Page & Sergey Brin (Google)

✔ Eric Schmidt (Google & Alphabet)

Despite his massive influence, Campbell wasn't a traditional executive. He was a coach at heart.

Bill Campbell's Coaching Philosophy

1. **Care deeply about people:** Campbell believed that leadership wasn't just about strategy, it was about people. He took the time to listen, support, and push his leaders to be their best.

2. **Ask, don't tell:** Instead of giving answers, he asked the right questions to help leaders think for themselves. His coaching wasn't about micromanaging; it was about empowering.

3. **Encourage risk-taking and learning from failure:** Campbell urged leaders to embrace bold ideas and learn from mistakes rather than fear failure.[85]

> *"Your title makes you a manager. Your people make you a leader."*
> **– Bill Campbell**

How to Apply Bill Campbell's Coaching Style

- **Build trust first** – Show people you care before coaching them.

- **Listen more than you talk** – Let them discover solutions through powerful questions.

- **Push people beyond their comfort zones** – Encourage growth through challenge and support.

If the greatest minds in tech needed a coach, imagine what coaching could do for your team.

Shift from "Telling" to "Asking"

Many leaders believe they need to have all the answers. However, great coaches understand that guiding someone to their own solution is far more powerful.

> *"A leader's job is not to have all the answers but to ask the right questions." - Simon Sinek*[86]

Exercise: Steps to Become a Coaching Leader

1. Start asking better questions

- Instead of: *"Why didn't you do this?"* Ask: *"What do you think got in the way?"*

- Instead of: *"Here's what you need to do."* Ask: *"What do you think would work best?"*

2. Dedicate time to coaching conversations

- Schedule one-on-one coaching sessions with your team members.

- Focus on growth, goals, and skill development (not just performance metrics).

3. Give feedback like a coach, not a critic

- Encourage strengths before addressing weaknesses.

- Use the SBI Model (Situation-Behavior-Impact) from Day 12 for constructive feedback.

4. Develop future leaders, not just employees

- Mentor your team and encourage leadership at all levels.

- Create an environment where people feel safe to take initiative, experiment, and grow.[8]

Final Leadership Principle: The Best Leaders Coach

At the highest level of leadership, your success is no longer measured by what you accomplish but by what you help others achieve.

"People don't grow when they're told what to do. They grow when they're challenged, encouraged, and supported." - Unknown[88]

Your leadership legacy won't be about how many tasks you managed. It will be about how many people you helped develop, inspire, and turn into leaders themselves.

Your Action Step For Today

- Coach one person today using the GROW Model.

- Ask more questions and give fewer instructions.

- Think about how you can develop leaders, not just manage tasks.

THE BEST LEADERS DON'T JUST GET THINGS DONE; THEY GROW THE PEOPLE AROUND THEM.

DAY 14: INFLUENCE WITHOUT AUTHORITY

THE REAL POWER BEHIND THE POSITION

"The key to successful leadership today is influence, not authority." –
Ken Blanchard[89]

Leadership is often associated with power, titles, and
decision-making authority. But true leadership is not about the
position you hold, it's about the influence you have. Some of
the most impactful leaders in history had no official power yet
changed the world through their ability to inspire, persuade, and
lead by example.

Think back to a time when you followed someone not because
you had to but because you wanted to. What made that person
compelling? Was it their knowledge? Their ability to listen? Their
vision? Whatever the reason, it likely came down to influence.

Influence vs. Authority: A Tale of Two Leaders

Sarah and James worked at the same company and had the same
goal of launching a new initiative to improve teamwork.

As a department head, Sarah assumed her title was enough to
get people on board. She sent out an email outlining her plan

and expected immediate compliance. But she faced resistance; people didn't fully understand the "why" behind the change, and without buy-in, the initiative stalled.

James, on the other hand, had no formal authority. But he built relationships, listened to concerns, and framed the idea as an opportunity rather than a directive. He shared relevant success stories, found early supporters, and slowly created momentum. In the end, James' initiative succeeded, not Sarah's, because he understood that influence, not authority, drives true leadership. So, how can you become more like James? It all comes down to your influence.

The 3 C's of Influence

1. Credibility: The Foundation of Trust

Influence begins with trust. If people don't believe in your character or expertise, they won't follow you. Warren Buffett, one of the world's most respected investors, has built his entire reputation on transparency. He openly admits his mistakes; something many leaders avoid. But by doing so, he earns trust. His investors believe in him not because he is perfect but because he is honest, reliable, and authentic.[90]

To build credibility:

- **Do what you say you'll do.** Even the smallest of broken commitments erode trust.

- **Be transparent.** Share challenges, not just successes.

- **Admit mistakes.** It strengthens, not weakens, your reputation.

2. Connection: The Power of Relationships

Influence isn't just about persuasion; it's about connection. People follow those they feel connected to. Oprah Winfrey built an empire not just through talent, but through her ability to deeply connect with people. She listens, empathizes, and makes every guest and audience member feel heard. This emotional connection makes her influence powerful.[91]

To build deeper connections:

- **Be genuinely curious about others.** Ask more questions than you answer.

- **Use people's names.** It fosters familiarity and respect.

- **Find common ground.** Before making a request, take time to build rapport.

3. Communication: The Art of Persuasion

To be influential, you must communicate in a way that moves people. Dr. Robert Cialdini, in his groundbreaking book *Influence: The Psychology of Persuasion*, identified six principles that make people more likely to say "yes."[92]

Cialdini's Six Principles of Influence:

1. **Reciprocity** – When you give first, people naturally want to give back.

2. **Commitment** – People stick to what they publicly commit to.

3. **Social Proof** – Show that others already support your idea.

4. **Authority** – Demonstrate expertise to gain credibility.

5. **Liking** – People follow those they like and relate to.

6. **Scarcity** – If something is rare, people value it more.

Steve Jobs was a master of persuasion. He didn't just sell products; he sold a vision. When recruiting talent, he didn't say, *"Come work for Apple."* Instead, he asked, *"Do you want to make a dent in the universe?"* That emotional appeal made people want to follow him.[93]

> **When you lead with credibility, connection, and communication, authority becomes irrelevant because people *choose* to follow you.**

Case Study: Mahatma Gandhi – The Ultimate Influencer

Mahatma Gandhi wielded significant influence despite lacking formal authority. He inspired and mobilized millions through non-violent resistance that played a crucial role in India's independence movement.[94]

Here's why Gandhi's influence was so powerful:

- **Moral Authority:** Gandhi's unwavering commitment to truth, non-violence, and justice resonated deeply with people, earning him immense respect and trust, even without holding any political office.

- **Inspiring Leadership:** He was a charismatic leader who could rally people to his cause, inspiring them to take action and challenge the British Raj through peaceful means.

- **Global Impact:** His philosophy and actions have had a profound impact on the world, inspiring movements for social justice and non-violent resistance in other countries.[95]

Gandhi's ability to influence events and shape public opinion, despite lacking any formal power, demonstrates the power of moral leadership and the ability to inspire people to act for a cause they believe in.

Exercise: Map Your Influence Network

To strengthen your ability to influence without authority, identify and develop key relationships in your workplace or industry.[96]

Step 1: Identify Key People

List 5-10 individuals who have influence in areas you care about. These could be colleagues, mentors, or leaders in your field.

Step 2: Build a Connection Strategy

For each person, ask yourself:

- How can I provide value to them?

- What common interests or goals do we share?

- What's one way I can strengthen this relationship?

Step 3: Take Action

Choose one person identified in step one and reach out, offer help, ask for advice, or simply express appreciation. Influence begins with connection.

Final Principle: Influence is Leadership in Action

The most powerful leaders don't rely on authority; they influence others through **credibility, connection, and communication**.

Action Steps For Today:

Try what is called the 3×3 Rule:

1. Give **three** unexpected compliments. (Make sure they are genuine.)

2. Help **three** people without expecting anything in return. (These can be simple tasks.)

3. Ask **three** open-ended questions to build a connection. (Build it into authentic conversations.)

INFLUENCE ISN'T NORMALLY ABOUT A SINGLE MOMENT; IT'S ABOUT CONSISTENTLY SHOWING UP, DELIVERING VALUE, AND BUILDING TRUST OVER TIME. REMEMBER, TRUE LEADERS DON'T DEMAND AUTHORITY; THEY EARN RESPECT.

Day 15: Conflict Resolution and Tough Conversations

Why Great Leaders Lean In, Not Away from Conflict

Conflict is uncomfortable, and most people avoid it at all costs; however, the best leaders don't avoid conflict, they welcome it. Think about the strongest teams, most successful companies, and greatest leaders. Are they perfect? No, they still have disagreements, tension, and tough conversations, but they have learned how to use those conflicts to strengthen their team and make it better.

"Peace is not the absence of conflict, but the ability to handle conflict by peaceful means." – Ronald Reagan[97]

If conflict is handled poorly, it can create division, resentment, and dysfunction. But when it is managed well, it can strengthen relationships, improve collaboration, drive innovation, and build trust. The key? Transforming conflict into productive conversations. If you want to be a great leader, learning how to navigate conflict is non-negotiable.[98]

Why Leaders Must Embrace Conflict

Many people think of conflict as a battle to be won, but strong leaders see it differently. Great leaders don't shy away from tough conversations. Instead, they:

- Listen before reacting

- Ask the right questions

- Focus on solutions, not blame

- Turn conflicts into learning opportunities

"A good leader doesn't avoid conflict; they embrace it with the intent to resolve and improve." – Simon Sinek[99]

A team without conflict is often a team that:

- Lacks innovation (because no one challenges ideas)

- Holds in frustration (until it explodes later)

- Settles for mediocrity (instead of pushing for excellence)

If you want a high-performing team, you need a healthy level of constructive conflict. The challenge is knowing how to navigate conflict effectively.

Exercise: The "5 Whys" Technique to Uncover the Root Cause

When a problem arises, it can be tempting to solve it only at the surface level. However, this approach never gets to the true root issue, which can cause more problems later. Dr. Sakichi Toyoda, the founder of Toyota, uses the "5 Whys" technique, a simple but powerful tool for getting to the root cause of a problem.[100]

How It Works:

When faced with a conflict or challenge, ask "Why?" five times to uncover the real issue.

Example: There is a team conflict over missed deadlines. Here is what the 5 Whys may look like in action.

- Why #1- Why did the deadline get missed? Because the team was overwhelmed with other projects.

- Why #2- Why was the team overwhelmed? Because they didn't have clear priorities.

- Why # 3- Why weren't priorities clear? Because leadership didn't set them.

- Why #4- Why didn't leadership set them? Because they assumed the team knew what was most urgent.

- Why #5- Why did they assume that? Because there wasn't clear communication.

So, what was the root cause? A lack of communication, not just missed deadlines. Once you identify the real problem, you can solve the right issue instead of just treating the symptoms.

Case Study: How Satya Nadella Transformed Microsoft's Toxic Culture

When Satya Nadella became CEO of Microsoft in 2014, he inherited a company full of conflict. Microsoft's culture was described as: "Cutthroat and combative, full of internal rivalries, and focused on individual wins instead of teamwork." Engineers and executives competed against each other instead of working with each other.[101]

Nadella's Leadership Shift: Turning Conflict into Collaboration

Instead of ignoring the toxic environment, Nadella tackled conflict head-on. Here's how:

- Shifted from a "know-it-all" to a "learn-it-all" culture

- Encouraged leaders to listen first, then respond

- Replaced a competitive mindset with a collaborative one

- Introduced open feedback loops to resolve tensions quickly

"Listen more than you talk. Respect others' ideas. Build on each other's strengths." – Satya Nadella

By addressing the real conflicts, Nadella helped Microsoft become one of the most respected and innovative companies in the world, all through better conflict resolution. If you want a high-performing team, don't avoid tough conversations. Create a culture where conflicts are handled with respect, curiosity, and collaboration.[102]

Want to navigate conflict like a pro?

Follow these action steps:

1. Separate People from the Problem: Conflict isn't personal; it's about an issue that needs to be solved. Instead of saying: *"You always miss deadlines."* Say: *"Let's figure out what's causing the delays and solve it together."*

2. Listen First, Then Speak: The best way to de-escalate conflict? Make the other person feel heard. You could ask: *"Can you tell me more about what's frustrating you?"*

3. Find Common Ground: There's always something to agree on, even in a disagreement. You could ask: *"What's one thing we both want to achieve here?"*

4. Focus on Solutions, Not Blame: Instead of wasting time deciding who is to blame, ask, *"How can we prevent this from happening again?"* You want to make sure you are moving forward in a solution. If not, you will get stuck in an endless cycle of the blame game.

5. Follow-up: Great leaders don't just resolve conflicts; they ensure lasting change. After a tough conversation, check-in and ask: *"How do you think things are going now?"* or *"Do you feel like we addressed the real issue?"*

The next time you face a tough conversation, apply these five steps. Watch how your leadership influence grows.

Final Leadership Principle: Conflict is an Opportunity, Not a Threat

At its core, conflict is not something to fear; it's something to embrace.

"Difficult conversations are uncomfortable, but avoiding them prevents growth." – Brené Brown[103]

Great teams don't avoid conflict. They:

- Use it to strengthen relationships

- Turn tension into trust

- Transform problems into solutions

Leaders who master conflict resolution create stronger teams, better cultures, and higher performance. So, the next time you're faced with a conflict, remember: It's not about winning or losing. It's about listening, learning, and leading.

Your Action Steps For Today:

- Identify a conflict you've been avoiding, and take one step to resolve it today.

- Use the "5 Whys" technique to uncover the real issue.

- Lead tough conversations with curiosity, respect, and a solution-focused mindset.

THE BEST LEADERS DON'T AVOID CONFLICT; THEY TRANSFORM IT. EVERY TOUGH CONVERSATION IS A CHANCE TO BUILD TRUST, UNCOVER TRUTH, AND LEAD WITH GREATER PURPOSE.

Day 16: Public Speaking and Communication Mastery

Why Great Leaders Inspire Through Words

Think about some of history's most impactful leaders: Martin Luther King Jr., Winston Churchill, Oprah Winfrey, and Steve Jobs. They all have one thing in common: **They know how to inspire through words.**

Public speaking is one of the most powerful leadership skills you can develop. Yet, for many, it's also the most terrifying.

You may be surprised to know that:

- The best speakers aren't naturally gifted; they practice.

- Powerful communication is a skill, not a talent.

- Anyone (even you) can master it.

Whether you're speaking to a small team or a large audience, your ability to communicate clearly and confidently will define your leadership success.

The Power of Words: A True Story

In 1963, on the steps of the Lincoln Memorial, Dr. Martin Luther King Jr. delivered one of the most iconic speeches in history: "I Have a Dream."[104] Imagine if he had said: *"I think equality is important, and we should work toward a better future."* Not quite as powerful as *"I have a dream,"* right? Dr. King's ability to paint a vision, evoke emotion, and captivate an audience made all the difference. Words matter. Delivery matters. And great leaders master both. You may not be delivering a speech to millions, but every conversation, meeting, and presentation is an opportunity to inspire.

The Biggest Public Speaking Myths (and the Truths Behind Them)

Before we dive into practical strategies, let's debunk a few myths:

Myth #1: Great speakers are born, not made.

Truth: Public speaking is a learned skill. Even the best speakers practiced relentlessly. I read a story not too long ago about a speaker preparing for a TED Talk. He practiced the speech as if he were giving it about 100 times!

Myth #2: More information makes for a better speech.

Truth: People don't remember facts; they remember stories and emotions.

Myth #3: You must be extroverted to be a great speaker.

Truth: Many top speakers are introverts who have developed strong communication skills.

Case Study: How Steve Jobs Mastered Public Speaking

Steve Jobs was not a natural speaker. In his early days at Apple, he was awkward, rushed, and unpolished. But over time, he transformed into one of the greatest presenters of all time.[105]

Here's how he did it, and what you can learn:

1. Simplicity is Power: Jobs didn't clutter his speeches with jargon. For Example: Instead of saying, *"The iPod is a revolutionary MP3 device with an ultra-compact form factor and state-of-the-art storage capacity,"* He said: **"1,000 songs in your pocket."** Simple. Memorable. Powerful.[106]

- **Leadership Lesson:** Speak in clear, simple messages people can remember.

2. Master the Power of the Pause: Most nervous speakers talk too fast. Jobs used pauses strategically to build anticipation and emphasize key points. For example: When introducing the iPhone, he paused before saying: *"And today... Apple is going to reinvent the phone."* Then the crowd erupted.[107]

- **Leadership Lesson:** Slow down. Use silence as a tool.

3. Tell Stories, Not Just Facts: Jobs didn't just list product features—he told compelling stories. For example, in his famous Stanford commencement speech, he told the deeply personal story of his cancer diagnosis and near-death experience. *"Remembering that you are going to die is the best way I know to avoid the trap of thinking you have something to lose."*[108] People don't remember numbers. They remember stories.

- **Leadership Lesson:** Make your message human and relatable.

If you can speak to hearts, you can move minds—and that's the essence of leadership.

How to Speak Like a Leader: Practical Steps

1. Start with a Strong Opening

- **Mistake:** Saying, *"Hi, my name is..."*

- **Better:** Start with a story, question, or bold statement.

2. Use the Rule of Three

- Our brains love patterns. That's why speeches with **three main points** are so effective.[109]

- Example: *"Great leaders do three things well: They listen, they inspire, and they take action."*

3. Speak with Energy and Passion

- **Mistake:** Talking in a monotone voice.

- **Better:** Vary your tone and show excitement.

4. End with a Memorable Call to Action: Your last words should leave an impact.

- **Weak Ending:** *"That's all I have. Thanks."*

- **Strong Ending:** *"If you want to be a great leader, start today by mastering your voice."*

Exercise: Record and Review a 2-Minute Leadership Speech

The best way to improve your speaking? **Watch yourself speak.**

- **Step 1:** Pick a leadership topic you're passionate about.

- **Step 2:** Record a 2-minute speech on your phone.

- **Step 3:** Watch the playback and take notes: Did you sound confident? Were your words clear and engaging? Did you use pauses effectively? Did your body language and facial expressions align with your message?

- **Step 4:** Do it again by improving one thing each time.

Final Leadership Principle: Master Your Message, Master Your Influence

Great leaders are great communicators. If you want to **inspire, lead, and influence**, you must:

- Learn to simplify complex ideas

- Use the power of stories and emotion

- Speak with confidence and clarity

Your Action Steps For Today:

- Record & review your 2-minute leadership speech.

- Apply one technique from today to improve your communication.

- Speak with clarity, confidence, and conviction, because your words have power.

LEADERSHIP IS INFLUENCE. AND INFLUENCE BEGINS WITH COMMUNICATION.

Day 17: Cultivating a Positive Work Culture

Why It Matters

What makes a workplace truly great? Is it high salaries? Perks like free coffee and gym memberships? Or is it something deeper? The answer is culture.

"The culture of any organization is shaped by the worst behavior the leader is willing to tolerate." -Gruenter & Whitaker[110]

Every leader wants a high-performing team, but the best teams don't thrive because of policies or processes alone. They thrive because of culture. Think of it as the invisible force that shapes everything from how people communicate to how they feel about their work. And as a leader, you set the tone.

The Hidden Power of Culture: A True Story

In 1982, Paul O'Neill took over as CEO of Alcoa, one of the world's largest aluminum manufacturers. Investors expected him to talk about profits and growth. Instead, his first speech stunned them. *"I want to talk to you about worker safety."* Silence. Confusion. Shareholders panicked. But O'Neill wasn't joking. He believed that a company's culture started with how it valued employees. He believed that focus would determine Alcoa's success. So, O'Neill made worker safety the company's #1 priority. If even a minor injury occurred, he expected an immediate report and a detailed plan to prevent it from happening again.[111]

What happened next?

Alcoa's workplace culture transformed.

- Employees felt valued and empowered.

- Communication and trust improved.

- Productivity and profits significantly increased.

O'Neill proved that when you get culture right, results follow.

Why Workplace Culture is a Competitive Advantage

Culture isn't just about making people happy; it's about driving business success.

- **Great culture reduces turnover.** Companies with strong cultures experience less burnout and up to 50% lower attrition rates.[112]

- **Great culture attracts top talent.** People want to work in environments where they feel respected, valued, and engaged.[113]

- **Great culture boosts performance.** Organizations with a strong culture outperform competitors by 20-30% in revenue growth.[114]

If you don't shape your culture intentionally, it will form accidentally' and that's risky.

Exercise: Identify One Small Cultural Improvement You Can Make Today

Step 1: Observe your current culture.

- What's working well?

- What's holding your team back?

Step 2: Choose one small, high-impact action to improve culture.

Here are a few examples:

- Start meetings with a positive shoutout for someone's contribution.

- Ask for feedback on workplace improvements.

- Celebrate wins (big or small) more frequently.

Step 3: Implement it today, not next week or next quarter – today.

- Culture isn't built overnight, but small daily actions shape long-term transformation.

Case Study: How Zappos Built a Culture-First Company

If there's one company famous for prioritizing culture, it's Zappos. Under CEO Tony Hsieh, Zappos became a global leader in customer service, not because of its products, but because of its culture.[115]

1. Core Values Are Everything

Zappos lives by **10 core values**; here are just a few:

- Deliver "WOW" through service

- Create fun and a little weirdness

- Pursue growth and learning

Lesson: Culture becomes random and inconsistent if your company doesn't define its values.

2. Culture Over Skills When Hiring

At Zappos, **cultural fit matters more than skills.**

- Every applicant goes through a "culture interview."

- If the applicant doesn't align with Zappos' values, they're not hired; even if they're highly skilled.

Lesson: You can teach skills, but you can't teach culture fit.

3. The "Pay to Quit" Test

This is unbelievable! After training, Zappos offers new employees **$2,000 to quit** if they don't love the culture.

- 97% of new hires stay because those who remain genuinely want to be there.

Lesson: A strong culture retains the right people and repels the wrong ones.

Practical Steps to Create a Positive Work Culture

1. Make People Feel Valued

- Mistake: Leaders only recognize big wins.

- Better: Regularly acknowledge small contributions.

- Example: A simple, *"I appreciate your hard work on that project"* builds a culture of appreciation.

2. Encourage Psychological Safety

- Mistake: Employees fear making mistakes.

- Better: Create a safe space for ideas, questions, and failure.

- Example: Google found that psychological safety (the freedom to take risks without fear) is the #1 factor of high-performing teams.[116]

3. Lead by Example

- Mistake: Leaders preach culture but don't live it.

- Better: Model the behaviors you want to see.

- Example: If you want a culture of transparency, be transparent yourself.

4. Foster a Sense of Purpose

- Mistake: Employees don't understand how their work matters.

- Better: Connect daily tasks to a bigger mission.

- Example: A hospital janitor who sees their job as *"helping save lives"* will be far more engaged than one who sees it as *"just cleaning floors."*

Final Leadership Principle: Culture is Built in the Small Moments

"Culture isn't just one thing. It's everything." -Tony Hsieh[117]

A thriving work culture isn't about one grand initiative; it's about consistent, small actions that build a strong foundation over time.

Your Action Steps For Today:

- Identify one cultural improvement you can make immediately.

- Implement it today.

- Lead by example, because culture starts with you.

THE CULTURE YOU WALK PAST IS THE CULTURE YOU ACCEPT.

Day 18: Delegation and Empowering Others

Why Great Leaders Don't Do It All

Many leaders struggle with delegation. They believe that if they want something done right, they have to do it themselves. But here's the problem: leaders who try to do everything end up leading nothing.

Think about it, if you're constantly bogged down in daily tasks, how will you ever have time for the big-picture thinking that leadership requires?

"If you want to go fast, go alone. If you want to go far, go together."
– African Proverb[118]

The best leaders don't just manage people; they develop them. They empower their teams, trust them with responsibility, and create an environment where others can step up and thrive.[119]

Real-World Story: The Leadership Trap

In her first few years as a principal, Anna was completely overwhelmed. She was the first to arrive every morning, the last to leave at night, and she handled everything, from hiring teachers to approving budgets to planning all the student and staff events. One day, a trusted mentor pulled her aside and said, *"You're not leading, you're managing every little detail. If you don't empower your team, you'll burn out, and they will never grow."*

That moment changed everything. She had been in *"get it done"* mode for so long that she forgot she was not on an island alone. From that day on, instead of doing everything herself, she started delegating responsibilities to department heads, trusting teachers to make decisions, and empowering her admin team to solve problems effectively.

The result?

- The school ran better and culture improved because people took ownership of their roles.

- Teacher engagement increased because they felt trusted.

- Anna finally had time to focus on being an effective instructional leader.

That's the power of delegation!

Why Delegation Is Essential

1. Delegation Builds Trust

When you delegate effectively, you show your team you trust them. And trust is the foundation of a high-performing team.

2. Delegation Develops Future Leaders

If you handle everything yourself, your team never learns how to lead. But if you give them responsibility, they gain the confidence and skills to step up.

3. Delegation Increases Efficiency

When leaders try to do everything, progress slows down. But when tasks are shared, work gets done faster and better.

4. Delegation Frees You for Strategic Thinking

The best leaders don't get stuck in the weeds. They focus on vision, strategy, and growth. To do that, they must learn how to delegate effectively.

"Don't tell people how to do things. Tell them what to do and let them surprise you with the results." – General George S. Patton[120]

Case Study: How Richard Branson Built Virgin by Trusting His Team

When you think of Virgin Group, you think of Richard Branson. But did you know that Branson doesn't run his companies? In fact, Branson credits delegation and empowerment as the key to Virgin's success.

- Branson hires the right leaders and then gets out of their way. He knows the best leaders don't control everything-they trust their team.

- Branson empowers his executives to make decisions without constantly seeking his approval. He knows when employees have ownership over decisions, they take greater responsibility.

- Branson believes in letting people fail and learn. He says, *"The best way to learn is by doing. Empower people to take risks, and they'll grow faster than you expect."*

The result? Virgin Group has over 400 companies, yet Branson spends his time on big-picture ideas, not daily operations. Why? Because he delegates.[121]

How to Delegate Effectively: 5 Practical Steps

1. **Start Small**-Start with one task and expand gradually. If you handle all team meetings, let a team member lead the next one.

2. **Delegate Outcomes, Not Just Tasks**-Explain the bigger goal, assign the task, and give your team ownership over the outcome (good or bad).

3. **Let Go of Perfectionism**-Thinking that no one can do it as well as you is a huge mistake. Accept that people will do things differently, but that's okay. Honestly, a different approach might actually lead to better results.

4. **Provide Feedback & Recognition**-Give support when needed, feedback along the way, and appreciation for their effort during and after the task is complete.

5. **Create a Culture of Ownership**-People should not feel as if they are just taking orders. Empower people to own their work and make decisions. Ask, *"How would you solve this problem?"* instead of giving them all the answers.[122]

Exercise: Delegate One Responsibility Using Clear Expectations

Step 1: Identify one task you're currently doing that someone else could handle. Ask yourself: *Does this require my unique expertise, or can I teach someone else to do it?*

Step 2: Choose the right person for the task. Consider skills, experience, and growth potential.

Step 3: Set clear expectations using the 5W1H Framework:[123]

- **What** needs to be done?

- **Why** is it important?

- **Who** is responsible?

- **When** is the deadline?

- **Where** should they focus their efforts?

- **How** should they approach it?

Step 4: Provide support, but don't micromanage. Be available for questions, but let them take ownership.

Step 5: Review the results and give constructive feedback.

Final Leadership Principle: Empowered Teams Create Stronger Leaders

"The function of leadership is to produce more leaders, not more followers." – Ralph Nader[124]

Too many leaders confuse being *in control* with being *in charge*. True leadership isn't about holding all the power; it's about giving it away with wisdom.

Delegation isn't a sign of weakness; it's a strategy for strength. It shows that you trust your team and believe in their ability to rise. Great leaders resist the urge to micromanage and instead coach, equip, and elevate the people around them.

Your Action Steps For Today:

- Identify **one task** to delegate.

- Choose the **right person** and set **clear expectations.**

- Let go, trust your team, and watch them thrive.

DELEGATION IS NOT A TASK; IT'S A TRUST. AND TRUST IS WHAT BUILDS TEAMS THAT LAST.

Day 19: The Servant Leadership Mindset

The Greatest Leaders Put Others First

Servant leadership flips the script in a world where leadership is often associated with power, status, and authority. Instead of asking, *"How can people serve me?"* great leaders ask, *"How can I serve others?"*

The best leaders don't lead for personal gain; they lead to lift others up. They prioritize their people, remove obstacles, and create environments where others can thrive.

The concept of servant leadership isn't new. Some of history's most influential leaders: Mahatma Gandhi, Mother Teresa, Nelson Mandela, and Abraham Lincoln, were servant leaders. They understood that true leadership isn't about dominance; it's about service.

Leadership isn't about titles, power, or authority. It's about service, sacrifice, and helping others grow.

The Restaurant Manager Who Led by Serving

A well-known restaurant chain was struggling with high employee turnover and low morale. Their general manager, Robert, decided to take a different approach. Instead of micromanaging from the office, Robert spent time on the floor, taking orders, washing dishes, and even helping clean up after closing. Employees were shocked. They weren't used to seeing a leader roll up their sleeves and work alongside them. But as days passed, something remarkable happened: Staff engagement increased, customer service improved dramatically, and turnover dropped significantly.

Why? Because Robert showed that leadership isn't about telling; it's about doing. By serving his employees, he inspired them to serve customers better. That's the essence of servant leadership.

Why Servant Leadership is Important

1. It Builds Unbreakable Trust

People follow leaders they trust. And trust is built not through words but through actions. When leaders serve their teams, they earn deep respect and loyalty.

> *"The best way to find yourself is to lose yourself in the service of others." – Mahatma Gandhi*[125]

2. It Creates a Culture of Collaboration

Servant leaders create a culture where everyone matters. When leaders value their people, employees become more engaged, more innovative, and more committed. Companies with strong servant leadership cultures, like Southwest Airlines and Chick-fil-A, have high employee retention, exceptional customer service, and strong financial success.

3. It Develops Stronger Future Leaders

Servant leaders don't just lead; they develop others to lead. When you mentor, coach, and invest in your team, they become better leaders themselves. For example, Howard Behar, former president of Starbucks, famously said: *"We're not in the coffee business serving people. We're in the people business serving coffee."*[126] He prioritized people first, profits second, and helped turn Starbucks into a global powerhouse.

Exercise: Commit One Act of Servant Leadership Each Day This Week

- **Step 1:** Identify one way to serve someone on your team each day this week.

- **Step 2:** Do it without expecting anything in return.

- **Step 3:** Reflect on the impact. Did it change how you felt about leadership?

Case Study: How Nelson Mandela Led Through Service

Few leaders in history embody servant leadership more than Nelson Mandela. Mandela didn't just fight for justice; he sacrificed his freedom for it, spending 27 years in prison for his efforts to end apartheid in South Africa. But here's what made Mandela a true servant leader:

- **He Put the Country Before Himself:** After being released from prison in 1990, he could have sought revenge. Instead, he preached forgiveness and unity.

- **He Led with Humility:** Despite being South Africa's first Black president, Mandela didn't cling to power. He served only one term, believing leadership is about service, not control.

- **He Created a Culture of Reconciliation:** Mandela worked tirelessly to unite black and white South Africans, using servant leadership to unite a divided nation.[127]

How to Adopt the Servant Leadership Mindset[128]

1. Listen More Than You Speak

- Seek to understand before seeking to be understood.

- Instead of giving quick advice, ask, *"What do you need from me?"*

2. Remove Obstacles for Your Team

- Don't expect your team to solve every problem alone. Ask how you can help remove barriers.

- If your team lacks resources, fight to get them what they need.

3. Lead by Example

- Model the values you want to see in others.

- If you want a hardworking team, be the hardest worker.

4. Make Decisions That Benefit the Whole, Not Just Yourself

- Make choices that serve the greater good rather than for personal gain.

- If a decision helps you but hurts your team, rethink it.

5. Lift Others Up

- Celebrate others' success instead of taking credit.

- When your team wins, make sure they get the spotlight.

Final Leadership Principle: Serve First, Lead Forever

"People don't care how much you know until they know how much you care." – John C. Maxwell[129]

Leadership isn't about being the loudest voice in the room; it's about listening, lifting others up, and showing up with humility every single day. If you want to lead in a way that truly matters, start by serving, because the most influential leaders are those who put others first.

Your Action Steps Today:

- Perform one act of servant leadership.

- Ask your team, "How can I support you?"

- Model service-first leadership in every interaction.

SERVANT LEADERSHIP DOESN'T DIMINISH YOUR AUTHORITY; IT AMPLIFIES YOUR IMPACT.

DAY 20: THE POWER OF GRATITUDE IN LEADERSHIP

WHY GRATITUDE IS A LEADERSHIP SUPERPOWER

In leadership, we focus so much on getting things done, being the best, and achieving results that we forget to stop and show gratitude: gratitude to those who helped us achieve the results and gratitude for having the opportunity to lead. If we overlook showing gratitude to others, over time, those we lead will feel we only see them as a means to an end instead of an integral part of the company. When you practice gratitude regularly, those you lead will show loyalty to you and your organization, gratitude towards others, and will see themselves as part of something bigger.

Great leaders understand that recognition isn't a luxury; it's a necessity. When people feel valued and appreciated, they are more engaged, more productive, and more committed to the leader and the organization.

"People work for money but go the extra mile for recognition, praise, and rewards." – Dale Carnegie[130]

Consider two different leaders:

Tod rarely acknowledges his team's efforts. He assumes they know that hard work is expected and thinks they don't need recognition. Over time, morale drops, employees feel unnoticed, and engagement declines.

Brandon understands the importance of gratitude. He regularly takes time to thank his team, recognizes their contributions, and celebrates wins. As a result, employees feel valued, trust their leader, and go the extra mile.

It is important to note that gratitude isn't just about saying *"thank you."* It's about creating a culture of appreciation where people feel seen, respected, and motivated to do their best.

The CEO Who Transformed a Company with Gratitude

Douglas Conant took over as CEO of Campbell Soup Company when it was struggling. Employee engagement was at an all-time low, and morale was declining. Instead of resorting to strict mandates or harsh directives, Conant chose a radically different approach; he made gratitude the foundation of his leadership.

Over his tenure, he wrote over 30,000 handwritten thank-you notes to employees. He personally recognized contributions, no matter how small.

He showed appreciation publicly and privately. The impact? Employee engagement soared, company performance improved, and trust in leadership increased. By leading with gratitude, Conant transformed Campbell's culture and results.

This story shows that small acts of appreciation can create a massive leadership impact.[131]

The Science of Gratitude in Leadership

Gratitude isn't just a feel-good concept; it's backed by science.

- **Gratitude Boosts Team Performance-**A study from the University of Pennsylvania found that when leaders express gratitude, team productivity increases by over 50%.[132]

- **Gratitude Improves Employee Retention-**Research from Glassdoor found that employees who feel unappreciated are twice as likely to leave their jobs.[133]

- **Gratitude Strengthens Relationships & Trust-**According to a Gallup study, employees who receive regular recognition are more engaged and loyal.[134]

Exercise: The Gratitude Letter Challenge

- **Step 1:** Choose three team members who have made an impact.

- **Step 2:** Write each person a handwritten letter expressing your appreciation.

- **Step 3:** Deliver the letters personally.

This simple act will strengthen relationships, boost morale, and deepen trust.

How Gratitude Saved a Failing Team

Kelly was a department manager at a rapidly growing marketing agency. While the company's success was exciting, the fast pace came at a cost; stress levels were high, employees were burned out, and turnover was rising. Instead of pushing her team harder, Kelly chose a different approach. She began each Monday meeting by thanking at least one employee for their contributions. She also encouraged team members to recognize and celebrate each other's efforts. Over time, gratitude became a core part of the team's culture. By the end of the year, job satisfaction had soared, productivity had improved, and turnover had dropped by 40%.

This proves that when leaders express gratitude, it transforms team culture.

Make Gratitude a Daily Leadership Habit

1. **Recognize Effort, Not Just Results:** Idea-Acknowledge the hard work and hours they put into a project.

2. **Make Gratitude Public and Private:** Idea-Create a record-keeping system for yourself to ensure you take time to show gratitude to each employee over time.

3. **Start and End Meetings with Gratitude:** Idea-Start each meeting with 60 seconds of gratitude.

4. **Create a Culture of Peer Recognition** Idea-Implement a "shout-out" system where employees recognize each other.

5. **Write One Gratitude Letter a Week:** Idea- Choose one person per week and send them a written note.

Final Leadership Principle: Gratitude is a Leadership Multiplier

"The deepest craving of human nature is the need to be appreciated."
- William James[135]

Gratitude isn't just a nice leadership trait; it's fundamental to a healthy culture. Leaders who make appreciation a core value see stronger teams, more engagement, higher loyalty, and better performance.

Your Action Steps For Today:

- Write **one gratitude letter** to a team member.

- Start your next meeting with **a moment of appreciation.**

- Make gratitude **a leadership habit.**

EVERY PERSON WANTS TO BE SEEN; GREAT LEADERS MAKE SURE THEY ARE.

PART 3

DAYS 21-30: LEADING FOR IMPACT

Day 21: Adaptive Leadership-Thriving in a Changing World

The One Leadership Skill That Matters More Than Ever

It may be tempting to follow the saying, *"If it's not broke, don't fix it,"* but in today's fast-paced world, you will quickly be left behind if you follow that advice. What worked 5 years ago may not work today. The ability to pivot (think of Ross from FRIENDS), adapt, and thrive under uncertainty separates great leaders from those who struggle.

"If you don't like change, you're going to like irrelevance even less." - *General Eric Shinseki* [136]

It is mind blowing to see how fast our world is changing around us. Things that we thought to be impossible 20 years ago are a reality today:

- AI is transforming work and decision-making.

- Remote and hybrid work models are disrupting traditional offices.

- Consumer behavior is shifting in due to global events. [137]

The leaders who will succeed in the future are not the ones who cling to old methods but those who embrace change with confidence and adaptability.

The Cost of Inflexibility

History is littered with examples of companies and leaders who refused to adapt and paid the price:

- Toys "R" Us ignored e-commerce and lost to Amazon.[138]

- Yahoo passed on buying Google for $1M, then faded into irrelevance.[139]

- Nokia dominated mobile phones until it failed to keep up with smartphones.[140]

Each of these companies had dominated the market at one point in time. Their downfall wasn't due to a lack of talent or resources. They simply couldn't (or wouldn't) adapt.

Now, let's look at a leader who embraced change and as a result caused his company to explode.

Case Study: How Brian Chesky Saved Airbnb by Adapting to Crisis

When the COVID-19 pandemic hit in 2020, Airbnb faced a disaster.[141]

- 80% of bookings were canceled overnight.

- The travel industry collapsed as countries shut down.

- Airbnb was on the brink of financial ruin.

What Most CEOs Would Have Done:

- Laid off employees without a plan.

- Cut costs at the expense of innovation.

- Waited for things to go "back to normal."

What Brian Chesky Did Instead:

- **He listened to customers.** Instead of pushing traditional vacations, Airbnb pivoted to local stays, helping people find escapes closer to home.

- **He supported hosts.** Airbnb launched new initiatives to help hosts earn income in different ways, including long-term stays and virtual experiences.

- **He stayed transparent.** Unlike most CEOs, Chesky held open meetings, admitted challenges, and shared clear plans with employees.[142]

The result?

- Airbnb rebounded faster than hotels and became profitable again within a year.

- Their stock significantly increased.

- The company emerged stronger and more innovative than before.

"A crisis is a time to act, not to freeze. If you don't adapt, you don't survive." – Brian Chesky[143]

The Science Behind Adaptive Leadership

So why do some leaders embrace change while others resist it? Psychologists have found that the key is adaptability. It is important to note that adaptability is a mindset, not just a skill.[144]

Remember Carolyn Dewitt's theory on Fixed vs. Growth Mindset?[145]

Here is what it may look like in the area of adaptability:

- **Fixed Mindset Leader:** *"This is how we've always done it."*

- **Growth Mindset Leader:** *"How can we do this better?"*

"Change is the end result of all true learning." – Leo Buscaglia[146]

Fun Fact: When leaders stay curious, challenge old beliefs, and seek new solutions, they train their brains to adapt faster. Why? Learning new things increases neuroplasticity in the brain.[147]

Exercise: How to Become a More Adaptive Leader

1. Get Comfortable with Uncertainty: Instead of waiting for perfect conditions before making decisions, accept that uncertainty is a part of leadership.

- **Try This:** Challenge yourself to make one quick decision today, even with limited information.

2. Stay Curious and Keep Learning: Don't assume what worked in the past will always work. Instead, view yourself as a learner, be open to new ideas (even crazy ones), and challenge your assumptions.

- **Try This:** Read one article each week on a new trend within your industry.

3. Experiment and Pivot Quickly: Instead of sticking to a plan you know is failing, be open and willing to change or even abandon it altogether if it is not working.

- **Try This:** Identify one current process or project needing adjustment and make the needed changes.

4. Surround Yourself with Different Perspectives: You will learn nothing and become stagnant if you only listen to and surround yourself with people who agree with you. Instead, seek out diverse opinions that will challenge your thinking.

- **Try This:** Ask someone with a different background or experience for their perspective on a key decision.

5. Lead with Transparency During Change: Instead of keeping employees in the dark about potential changes (thinking you are protecting them), trust them with the information, over-communicate, and share the "why."

- **Try This:** The next time a major change is coming, involve your team early in the process.

Real-World Story: The Restaurant That Adapted and Thrived

In 2020, Fat Rice, a small family-owned restaurant in Chicago, was on the verge of closing due to the pandemic. Instead of accepting defeat, the owner:

- Created meal kits so families could cook their favorite restaurant dishes at home.

- Offered online cooking classes to generate new income.

- Partnered with local businesses to create bundled meal-and-grocery packages.

The result? Not only did revenue increase, but it also gained new customers. This is what adaptable leadership looks like: seeing possibilities instead of obstacles.[148]

Final Leadership Principle: Adaptability is the New Competitive Advantage

"The illiterate of the 21st century will not be those who cannot read and write, but those who cannot learn, unlearn, and relearn." – Alvin Toffler[149]

If you want to thrive as a leader, make adaptability your greatest strength. Stay open to change and challenge outdated assumptions. Pivot quickly when necessary.

Your Action Steps For Today:

- Identify **one change you've been resisting.**

- Find **one small way to embrace it today.**

- Reflect on **how adaptability can make you a stronger leader.**

IN TODAY'S WORLD, THE MOST RELEVANT LEADERS ARE THE ONES WHO EVOLVE FASTER THAN THE PROBLEMS THEY FACE.

Day 22: Resilient Leadership-The Power of Mental Toughness

Why Mental Toughness is the Secret to Lasting Leadership

Every leader faces adversity, setbacks, and moments of doubt. The difference between those who crumble under pressure and those who rise stronger comes down to resilience.

"Do not pray for an easy life. Pray for the strength to endure a difficult one." - Bruce Lee[150]

Resilient leaders don't avoid hardship; they learn to navigate it, grow from it, and inspire others in the process. When you think of great leaders, you probably admire their confidence, decisiveness, and vision. But behind every strong leader is a foundation of resilience; the mental toughness to keep moving forward, no matter the challenge.

Resilience in Action: The Airline Captain Who Saved 155 Lives

On January 15, 2009, Captain Chesley "Sully" Sullenberger was piloting US Airways Flight 1549 when both engines failed after a bird strike, just minutes after takeoff.[151]

With zero engine power, he had seconds to decide what to do.

- He didn't panic. He stayed calm, assessed his options, and communicated with air traffic control.

- He ignored distractions. While others might have hesitated or overthought the situation, he trusted his training and instincts.

- He made the impossible decision. With no time to reach an airport, Sully executed an emergency landing on the Hudson River, a feat never done successfully before.

- He put others first. After the landing, Sully personally walked through the aircraft twice to ensure every passenger was safely evacuated.

- The result? All 155 people on board survived.

His story is a perfect example of resilient leadership, staying calm, thinking clearly, and leading under extreme pressure.

Resilience isn't just about making it to the other side of difficulty; it's about developing the skills needed to turn adversity into growth.

4 Traits of a Resilient Leader

1. Emotionally Stable

Resilient leaders don't let emotions cloud their judgment. They stay level-headed under pressure. They are able to remain calm and make strategic decisions.[152]

- **Simple Tip:** The next time you feel stressed, pause for 10 seconds before responding. This simple habit prevents impulsive, emotionally driven decisions.

2. Able to Adapt in the Middle of a Crisis

A resilient leader doesn't see setbacks as dead ends; they see them as detours to something greater.[153]

- **Simple Tip:** When you are in the middle of a challenge, think about what you can learn from the situation. Instead of focusing on the obstacle, focus on the lesson.

3. Have Unshakable Optimism

Resilient leaders maintain hope and confidence even when things seem impossible. They inspire others by seeing possibilities instead of problems.[154]

- **Simple Tip:** When facing a challenge, list three possible solutions instead of fixating on what's wrong.

4. Know the Importance of a Strong Support System

No leader succeeds alone. Resilient leaders lean on mentors, peers, and teams for strength and perspective.[155]

- **Simple Tip:** Identify one person you consider a mentor. If you don't have one, find one. Remember, asking for help is not a sign of weakness; it's a sign of strength.

In moments of extreme stress, your brain reacts in three ways: fight, flight, or freeze mode. Have you ever heard of "Leader Mode"? Probably not, because it's not a thing, but if it were, it could be defined as focused, decisive, and strategic. **You have the ability to control your stress.**

The 3 Step "Stress Shield" Technique helps you stay Clear-Headed Under Pressure:

- Step 1: Breathe with Intention: Slow your breathing. Inhale for 4 seconds, hold for 4 seconds, exhale for 6 seconds. Repeat 3 times. This calms your nervous system.[156]

- Step 2: Ask a Power Question: Instead of asking, "Why is this happening?" ask, "*What's my best move right now?*" This will shift your brain into problem-solving mode.[157]

- Step 3: Act Decisively: Take one small action immediately, even if it's just writing down a plan. Why? Because action builds momentum.[158]

Case Study: How Vera Wang Built an Iconic Fashion Empire from Failure

Before becoming a fashion designer, Vera Wang faced two major career setbacks. Did you know Wang trained as a competitive figure skater for years, dreaming of making the U.S. Olympic team? Despite her dedication, she didn't make the team. Later, she spent 17 years climbing the ranks at Vogue, becoming a senior fashion editor. But when the Editor-in-Chief position opened, she was passed over for the top job. Heartbroken, she left Vogue, a decision that ultimately led her to reinvent herself and become one of the world's most iconic fashion designers.[159]

Her response? Instead of seeing these failures as the end, Wang pivoted and found a new path.

- At age 40, she started her own bridal fashion brand with zero experience in business.

- She learned, adapted, and persisted through multiple financial setbacks.

- Today, Vera Wang is one of the most successful designers in the world.

"Success isn't about avoiding failure. It's about refusing to be stopped by it." – Vera Wang[160]

Her story is proof that setbacks don't define your future; your response does.

Exercise: Reflect on a Difficult Period in Your Life

Think of a moment in your life when you faced significant difficulty.

Step 1: What was the challenge?

Step 2: How did you respond at the time?

Step 3: What lesson did you learn from it?

Step 4: How can you apply that lesson to your life today?

This exercise can help you reframe difficult times in your life, and these same steps can be applied to your leadership growth.

Final Leadership Principle: Resilience is a Choice

It is important to note that resilience does not mean you have no fear. It simply means you know how to face fear and overcome it.

To Sum it Up:

- When stress hits, stay calm and focused.

- When setbacks come, find the lesson, not the excuse.

- When failure happens, pivot and push forward.

As Reepicheep says in *The Chronicles of Narnia: The Voyage of the Dawn Treader* (2010), *"Hardships often prepare ordinary people for an extraordinary destiny."* [161]

Your Action Steps For Today:

- Identify one challenge you're currently facing.

- Apply the "Stress Shield" Technique next time you need to stay clear-headed in a stressful situation.

- Apply one of the tips from the "4 Traits of a Resilient Leader" section.

YOU DON'T BECOME A GREAT LEADER IN COMFORT; YOU BECOME ONE IN THE MOMENTS YOU CHOOSE COURAGE OVER FEAR, AND GRIT OVER GIVING UP.

DAY 23: THE LEADERSHIP EDGE-BUILDING STRATEGIC THINKING SKILLS

WHY STRATEGIC THINKING SEPARATES GOOD LEADERS FROM GREAT ONES

In leadership, it's easy to get caught up in the day-to-day demands, responding to emails, putting out fires, and handling immediate issues. But great leaders don't just react to what's happening now; they think ahead, try to anticipate obstacles, and position their organization for future success.

Strategic thinking is the key to long term success.[162] Your ability to see beyond the present and make calculated decisions determines whether you thrive or struggle.

But here's the challenging part: most leaders are trained to be tactical, not strategic. Tactical thinking solves immediate problems, while strategic thinking prepares for future challenges and opportunities. Both are critical in leadership, but without strategic thinking, you can get stuck in a cycle of reacting instead of leading.

The Difference Between Tactical and Strategic Thinking

Tactical Thinking (Short-Term Focus)

- Solves immediate problems

- Focuses on execution

- Reacts to what's happening right now

- Measures quick wins

Strategic Thinking (Long-Term Vision)

- Anticipates future challenges

- Focuses on big-picture goals

- Plans proactively instead of reacting

- Builds a roadmap for sustainable success

Great leaders can balance both types of thinking. They solve today's challenges while preparing for tomorrow's opportunities.

Strategic Thinking in Action: How a Chess Grandmaster Outsmarted His Opponent

In 1997, world chess champion Garry Kasparov faced off against Deep Blue, an IBM supercomputer. At the time, Kasparov was the undisputed greatest human chess player. But Deep Blue had something Kasparov didn't; the ability to calculate 200 million positions per second.

From a tactical standpoint, Kasparov had no chance of out-calculating a machine. So how did he compete? He played strategically.

Instead of matching Deep Blue's brute-force calculations, Kasparov focused on long-term positioning. He made moves that didn't necessarily win in the short term but set him up for a stronger advantage in the later stages of the game. What can we learn from this? Success isn't about making the quickest moves; it's about making the right moves that set you up for long-term victories.[163]

"Tactics is knowing what to do when there is something to do. Strategy is knowing what to do when there is nothing to do." – Savielly Tartakower[164]

The next time you're faced with a decision, ask yourself: *"Am I just reacting, or am I setting up for future success?"*

Exercise: 3 Strategies that Can Sharpen Your Strategic Mindset:

Strategy 1: Think in "What If" Scenarios[165]

Great strategists don't just focus on what's happening now; they think about what could happen next. The next time you're making a decision, ask yourself these three questions:

1. *What are three possible ways this situation could unfold?*

2. *What if this decision doesn't work? What's my backup plan?*

3. *What will this choice look like in six months or a year?*

Why this works? It forces you to anticipate obstacles before they happen instead of scrambling to fix them later.

Strategy 2: Zoom Out and See the Big Picture[166]

When leaders are stuck in the details, they may miss the real issue at hand. Follow the steps below to zoom out:

1. Identify the Big Picture-Ask:W*hat is the overarching issue?*

2. Break the Problem Into Parts-Ask:W*hat main areas contribute to this problem?*

3. Find the Root Cause-Ask:*Why? Use* 5he 5 Whys method from day 15.

4. Focus on the one or two biggest issues instead of getting lost in minor details.

5. Now that you've identified the core issue, break it into smaller, immediate steps.

6. Monitor and Adjust until the problem is solved.

Why This Works: It shifts your focus from putting out fires to problem-solving, ensuring you take action before small challenges turn into major setbacks.

Strategy 3: Challenge Your Own Assumptions ("Red Teaming")[167]

One of the biggest mistakes leaders make is assuming their decisions are right without testing them or trying to prove why they are wrong or won't work. "Red Teaming" is a military strategy that intentionally challenges decisions by examining them from multiple perspectives. It forces you to confront weaknesses and potential failures that might have been ignored due to excitement or overconfidence. Here's how to do it:

- Pick an important decision you're about to make.

- List three arguments against your decision.

- Ask: *"If I were my biggest competitor, how would I pick this strategy apart or try to make it fail?"*

Why This Works: It forces you to identify blind spots before they become failures.

"Strategy without reflection is just luck." – Unknown[168]

Case Study: How Angela Merkel Used Strategic Thinking to Navigate Global Crises

Angela Merkel, Germany's first female chancellor, served for 16 years and became a well-respected world leader. But what made Merkel stand out wasn't just her intelligence; it was her exceptional ability to think strategically.

How She Used Strategic Thinking to Lead:

- The Eurozone Crisis (2008-2012): While other European leaders reacted emotionally to the financial collapse, Merkel took a calculated approach, balancing economic aid with financial discipline.[169]

- The Refugee Crisis (2015): When millions of refugees fled war-torn regions, Merkel didn't just react—she anticipated long-term consequences and developed policies that helped integrate over 1 million refugees.[170]

- The COVID-19 Pandemic (2020): Merkel relied on science-driven, long-term strategies instead of short-term political moves, leading Germany to one of the lowest fatality rates in Europe.[171]

Her ability to see beyond short-term politics and make difficult, forward-thinking decisions is what made her one of the most effective global leaders of the 21st century.

Final Leadership Principle: Strategy Wins Over Reaction

"Failing to plan is planning to fail." - Unknown[172]

A leader who only reacts will always be playing catch-up.

Remember:

- Think beyond today and anticipate tomorrow.

- Challenge your own decisions and find blind spots before they hurt you.

- Balance short-term execution with long-term vision.

Your Action Steps For Today:

- Take one upcoming decision and apply one of the strategies in this chapter.

- Identify **at least one blind spot** in your thinking.

- Adjust your strategy **before problems arise.**

LEAD LIKE A CHESS MASTER; NOT JUST FOR YOUR NEXT MOVE, BUT FOR THE CHECKMATE.

Day 24: Psychological Safety-Creating an Environment Where Teams Thrive

The Foundation of High-Performing and Resilient Teams

Picture two very different workplaces:

- In the first workplace, employees hesitate to speak up in meetings. They worry that their ideas will be dismissed, that asking questions will make them look incompetent, or that challenging those in leadership will have consequences. Mistakes are hidden instead of discussed because no one wants to be blamed. Over time, creativity stagnates, trust erodes, and the best employees leave for healthier work environments.

- Now, imagine the second workplace. Here, employees freely share ideas without fear of judgment. They feel safe asking questions, raising concerns, and admitting when they need help. Leadership actively listens and encourages different perspectives. Mistakes aren't punished but are seen as learning opportunities. The result? Innovation thrives, teamwork is strong, and employees are deeply engaged.

The difference between these two teams isn't talent or resources; **it's psychological safety.**

"Psychological safety is not about being nice. It's about giving candid feedback, openly admitting mistakes, and learning from each other."
– Amy Edmondson, Harvard Business School[173]

Psychological safety is the belief that you won't be punished, humiliated, or ignored for expressing your thoughts, taking risks, or making mistakes. Without psychological safety, people stay silent. With it, teams reach their full potential.[174]

This isn't just theory; it's backed by data. Google's landmark Project Aristotle study found that the highest-performing teams weren't the ones with the most talented individuals but the ones where members felt safe to express themselves.[175]

As a leader, your job isn't just to drive results; it's to create an environment where people feel empowered to contribute their best thinking.

The 3 Pillars of a Psychologically Safe Workplace

1. Trust – Creating a Foundation of Security

Trust is the bedrock of psychological safety. When employees trust their leader, they believe:

- Their voice matters.
- They won't be ridiculed or punished for mistakes.
- Leadership values their input.

Example: Google's "Project Aristotle"

Google spent years studying its highest-performing teams to figure out what made them so effective. The most important factor? Psychological safety. When employees felt safe speaking up, taking risks, and sharing ideas, their teams thrived. When they didn't, performance suffered, even if the team had top-tier talent.[176]

Leadership Tip: Build trust by admitting your own mistakes. When leaders show vulnerability, employees feel safer doing the same.

"Vulnerability is not weakness. It is our greatest measure of courage." – Brené Brown[177]

2. Respect – Welcoming Diverse Perspectives

A culture of respect means every idea is heard and valued, even if it's not implemented.

Example: NASA's Challenger Disaster

In 1986, NASA engineers warned leadership that the space shuttle Challenger had a serious defect. However, because NASA had a culture that discouraged dissent, these concerns were ignored. The result? The Challenger exploded just 73 seconds after liftoff, killing all seven astronauts aboard; a tragedy that could have been prevented.[178]

This example shows why leaders must actively invite different perspectives. If team members don't feel safe raising concerns, there's a real risk of overlooking major problems.

Leadership Tip: Before making key decisions, ask: *"What are we missing?"* or *"Is there anyone who disagrees? Why?"* Encouraging constructive debate leads to better decisions and prevents costly mistakes.

3. Open Communication – Making It Safe to Speak Up

A psychologically safe environment is one where employees feel comfortable sharing thoughts, ideas, and concerns.[179]

"Leaders who don't listen will eventually be surrounded by people who have nothing to say." – Andy Stanley[180]

Example: Microsoft's "Learn-It-All" Culture

Before Satya Nadella became CEO, Microsoft had a cutthroat, competitive culture where admitting mistakes was seen as weakness.[181]

Nadella transformed the culture by encouraging employees to:

- Ask questions instead of pretending to know everything.

- Admit when they were wrong and focus on learning.

- Speak up in meetings without fear of judgment.

The result? Microsoft became one of the world's most innovative companies.

Leadership Tip: Ask your team members:

- *"What's one thing we could improve?"*

- *"What's something you've been afraid to say?"*

This simple act makes employees feel heard and valued.

Case Study: How Pixar Built a Fearless Feedback Culture

Pixar is one of the most successful creative companies in history. But it wouldn't have thrived without a culture that made it safe to challenge ideas.

- The Problem: Early on, Pixar leaders realized that employees stayed silent when they saw flaws in projects. People feared upsetting higher-ups, so they didn't voice concerns.

- The Solution: Pixar co-founder Ed Catmull introduced Braintrust Meetings, where anyone could critique a project, including junior employees.

The Result:

- Employees felt safe to challenge ideas.

- This led to constant improvements, turning weak ideas into masterpieces.

- Pixar went on to produce 14 consecutive box office hits.[182]

Leadership Lesson: Fear kills creativity. The best teams make it safe to challenge ideas, not just agree with leadership.

Exercise: How Safe Does Your Team Feel?

Want to assess your team's psychological safety? Try this simple exercise.

1. Ask your team anonymously: *"On a scale of 1-10, how safe do you feel speaking up?"* and *"What's one thing leadership*

could do to make it safer?"

2. Listen without defending or justifying.

3. Make one change based on feedback.

Why This Works: Employees won't speak up unless they see action. Making even one small change builds trust.

Final Leadership Principle: Safety Fuels Success

"People don't fear hard work. They fear punishment for taking risks."
– Unknown

A team that feels safe to speak up, challenge ideas, and take risks will always outperform a team that stays silent out of fear.

- Trust your team enough to listen.

- Respect diverse opinions, even if they challenge you.

- Create a culture where mistakes lead to learning, not punishment.

Your Action Steps For Today:

- Ask one team member, *"What's one thing we could improve?"*

- **Listen without interrupting.**

- Take action, **even if it's small.**

YOU CAN'T UNLOCK YOUR TEAM'S FULL POTENTIAL UNTIL YOU UNLOCK THEIR VOICE.

Day 25: The Science of Energy Management-Avoiding Burnout in Leadership

The Secret to Leading Well Without Running on Empty

In the fast-paced world of leadership, many of us become obsessed with managing time. We're constantly trying to squeeze more tasks into the day, using every minute to its fullest, but time management alone won't make you effective as a leader. It's energy management that fuels your ability to perform at your highest level.

Have you ever found yourself working late into the night, staring at your screen, but feeling mentally drained and physically exhausted? Have you felt emotionally spent, unable to come up with the motivation to inspire or lead your team? When you're exhausted, mentally or emotionally, it's nearly impossible to lead your team effectively. That's because energy is the true currency of high-performance leadership.

"Energy, not time, is the fundamental currency of high performance."
– Tony Schwartz, The Energy Project[183]

Leaders often focus on managing their time, but what really matters is managing their energy.

4 Types of Energy Every Leader Must Optimize

Energy isn't just about staying awake and alert. It's about managing and replenishing four distinct energy sources, each of which plays a vital role in your effectiveness as a leader.[184]

1. Physical Energy – The Foundation of Vitality

Physical energy is the most basic form of energy, yet it's often the one we neglect the most. If you don't take care of your body, your mind and emotions will quickly follow suit. To perform at your best, you need to ensure that your body is well-rested, nourished, and exercised.

Example: Richard Branson's Daily Routine

Richard Branson, founder of Virgin Group, is notorious for his early morning workouts. He wakes up at 5 a.m. to go for a jog or kite surf. Branson says that physical exercise gives him the energy and mental clarity he needs to make big decisions and lead with creativity.[185]

Physical energy improves productivity and allows you to engage fully in other aspects of leadership, like problem-solving and interpersonal communication.

Leadership Tip: Commit to 30 minutes of exercise, even if it's a brisk walk. Pay attention to how you feel before and after.

2. Mental Energy – Staying Focused and Sharp

Mental energy refers to your ability to concentrate, solve problems, and think critically. Leaders who are constantly "on" or juggling tasks may feel mentally drained by the end of the day, reducing their ability to focus on high-priority decisions.

Example: Cal Newport's Deep Work Philosophy

Cal Newport, computer science professor and bestselling author, is well-known for his practice of "deep work." He carves out long, distraction-free blocks of time to focus intensely on complex tasks. Instead of constantly reacting to emails or minor tasks, he deliberately protects his mental energy by dedicating time to uninterrupted thinking and problem-solving. This habit helps him stay sharp, make better decisions, and maintain a high level of creativity and productivity.[186]

Mental energy requires focused time blocks when you're free from distractions and can give your full attention to the most important tasks.

Leadership Tip: Identify a time during your day when you can block out distractions and dedicate 30 minutes to deep work. Whether it's writing, strategizing, or solving a complex issue, guard this time fiercely to recharge your mental energy.

3. Emotional Energy – Maintaining Positive Relationships

Many leaders believe they have to hide emotions to appear strong. But Brené Brown's research proves that embracing emotions, rather than suppressing them, leads to stronger leadership. Instead of burning out by pretending to *have it all together,"* she encourages leaders to:

- Acknowledge emotional exhaustion instead of ignoring it.

- Communicate openly with teams about challenges.

- Lead with authenticity, not perfection.

Leaders who don't manage their emotional energy risk becoming overwhelmed, burnt out, or detached. Emotional intelligence is critical to effective leadership, especially during stressful times.[187]

Leadership Tip: Take a moment today to reflect on your emotions; what are you feeling? How can you recharge emotionally? Consider engaging in a mindfulness practice or having an honest conversation with a colleague.

4. Purpose Driven Energy – Fueling Passion and Motivation

Purpose-driven energy is the emotional and spiritual drive that keeps you going during tough times. This form of energy is rooted in your sense of purpose and your alignment with values and goals. When you lead with purpose, your energy feels limitless, and setbacks seem like temporary challenges rather than roadblocks.

Example: Elon Musk's Vision for Mars

Elon Musk's passion for colonizing Mars drives his incredible energy to innovate and push boundaries. Musk openly admits that he's driven by a larger purpose: to ensure the survival of humanity by making life multi-planetary. This sense of mission fuels his work ethic and propels him through adversity.[188]

Purpose-driven energy is the most sustainable type of energy because it's deeply tied to your personal values and vision for the future. When your leadership aligns with a sense of purpose, you inspire others and recharge yourself at the same time.

Leadership Tip: Take 10 minutes today to reflect on your deeper "why" as a leader. What drives you? What mission or vision fuels your leadership journey? Reconnect with this purpose when you feel drained.

Exercise: Identifying Energy Drains and Energizing Habits

One of the most powerful actions you can take to optimize your energy is identifying the habits that drain it, and then replacing them with revitalizing ones.

- **Identify the energy drain:** Reflect on your daily habits. Which activities leave you feeling exhausted, frustrated, or mentally foggy?

- **Replace the drain with an energizing habit:** What's one positive habit you can add to your routine? Consider physical exercise, reading, taking breaks in nature, or spending time with loved ones.

"You don't have to be perfect, just consistent." – *James Clear*[189]

Case Study: Arianna Huffington and Her Leadership After a Burnout Collapse

In 2007, Arianna Huffington, co-founder of The Huffington Post, experienced a life-changing event: she collapsed from exhaustion after working long hours without proper sleep. The experience led her to rethink her approach to leadership and personal well-being.

Huffington realized that her leadership, driven by constant hustle, had drained her physically and emotionally. After the collapse, she dedicated herself to promoting wellness and energy management as core components of leadership. (We will read about what she did next on Day 30.)[190]

Leadership Lesson: Leaders who burn the candle at both ends may achieve short-term success, but the long-term impact is often unsustainable.

Final Leadership Principle: Leadership is a Marathon, Not a Sprint

Managing your energy is about **sustainable performance** over time. Leadership isn't about pushing yourself to the breaking point; it's about being **strategic** with how you distribute your energy across the four key areas: physical, mental, emotional, and purpose-driven.

> **Your Action Steps For Today:**
>
> - **Identify** areas that are draining your energy.
>
> - **Apply** at least one leadership tip from the "Four Types of Energy Every Leader Must Optimize" section.

MAKE ENERGY MANAGEMENT A PART OF YOUR DAILY ROUTINE, AND WATCH YOUR LEADERSHIP SOAR!

Day 26: Crisis Leadership-How to Stay Calm Under Pressure

Leading in Crisis: The Real Test of Leadership

Leadership is often seen as a smooth, continuous path of growth, development, and forward motion. However, the true measure of a leader doesn't come during calm and steady times; it comes during moments of crisis when the stakes are high, emotions run wild, and the outcome hangs in the balance. In times of uncertainty, the quality of your leadership is tested, and your actions are scrutinized. People don't just remember the decisions you make; they remember how you made them feel during the most chaotic moments.

When a crisis strikes, it's easy to become overwhelmed by the gravity of the situation. The pressure mounts and everything seems urgent. The most effective leaders don't panic. Instead, they act with decisiveness, transparency, and a steady hand. They have the emotional intelligence to stay calm, focus on what's important, and inspire confidence in others, even when the situation seems dire.

The best crisis leaders possess a rare combination of clarity, calmness, and confidence, which helps their team stay focused, make better decisions and navigate the storm.

The 4 Phases of Crisis Leadership

Effective crisis leadership is not just about reacting in the moment; it's about being prepared and having a strategy that addresses every crisis stage. When you break it down, crisis leadership consists of 4 distinct phases: Preparation, Response, Communication, and Recovery. Each phase requires different approaches and skills, but the ultimate goal is to guide your team or organization through the storm and back to safety.[191]

1. Pre-Crisis: Preparedness – The Calm Before the Storm

The most effective crisis leaders don't wait for a crisis to unfold before they take action. Instead, they are proactively preparing for the worst-case scenarios, anticipating potential issues, and crafting strategies for the "what-ifs." Preparation is key because it gives you the framework and mindset to stay calm when a crisis strikes.

The key to preparation is training and simulation. Having a clear set of action steps, roles, and a plan can give you confidence during a crisis. This phase may include emergency response drills, establishing clear communication channels, and even running through hypothetical scenarios with your team. By preparing for the worst, you will feel more in control when a real crisis occurs.

2. Crisis: Decisiveness in the Moment

Assess, Activate, Alert: When a crisis hits, decisiveness is critical. In these moments, leaders can't afford to hesitate. Swift action, even if imperfect, is better than no action at all. While you may not have all the information or certainty, you need to make decisions based on the best available data and adapt as new information comes in.

Leaders must manage the response phase by taking charge and assigning roles. People look to leaders for direction, so remaining calm and maintaining confidence will help your team trust your decisions. The quicker the response, the more likely you can contain the damage and minimize the long-term impact.

3. Response: Action, Reassurance, and Communication – Keeping Everyone Informed

This is the stage where things are moving fast, and action plans are in place. During a crisis, communication becomes a powerful tool. Miscommunication can lead to confusion, panic, and a breakdown of trust. One of the most vital things you can do as a leader is to keep people informed, no matter how difficult the news may be. Transparency and clarity are critical during this phase, as it allows people to understand what's happening, why it's happening, and what they need to do.[192]

In a crisis, over-communication is better than under-communication. Constant updates, even when the news isn't ideal, help to create a sense of control and confidence. People need to hear from you, not just from rumors or second-hand sources. Consistency is key.

4. Recovery: Moving Beyond the Crisis

Once the immediate crisis is over, recovery begins. The recovery phase is about restoring normalcy, supporting your team through the aftermath, and learning lessons from the experience. After a crisis, it's important to debrief, analyze the response, and identify areas for improvement.

The recovery phase is also where you begin the work of rebuilding morale and trust. People may be emotionally drained, so showing empathy, providing support, and helping everyone find a way forward will be essential to bringing your organization back to stability.

Exercise: Write a "Crisis Playbook"

One of the most important things you can do today is to develop a "Crisis Playbook", a set of guidelines and actions for responding to a hypothetical challenge in your industry. This playbook will give you a proactive approach to handling potential crises, ensuring you are ready when the real deal hits. Most companies already have procedures and plans; if that is the case, make sure you are familiar with the procedures and are clear on what they look like for the company or department you lead. I can tell you firsthand that the thought, "*That will never happen here.*" is a naive way to lead. Be prepared and know what to do. You are the leader, the one people will be looking to, so make sure you are prepared.[193]

Here's how to structure your playbook:

1. Identify the potential crisis: This could be anything from a data breach, a public relations issue, a financial setback, or even a global crisis like a pandemic.

2. Outline the key players: Who needs to be involved? Who is responsible for each phase of the response?

3. Develop the communication plan: What messages will need to go out to employees, customers, the public, etc.?

4. Define your priorities: What are the most important actions to take in the first 24 hours, and what can wait?

Case Study: How Captain Richard de Crespigny Saved Qantas Flight 32

Great crisis leaders don't panic; they assess, adapt, and act under pressure. One of the best modern examples of crisis leadership in action is Captain Richard de Crespigny, the pilot of Qantas Flight 32, who successfully landed a severely damaged aircraft and saved 469 lives.

The Crisis: Mid-Air Explosion

On November 4, 2010, Qantas Flight 32 took off from Singapore, heading to Sydney. Shortly after takeoff, one of the Airbus A380's four engines exploded mid-air, causing a catastrophic failure that damaged key flight systems, punctured the fuel tanks, and knocked out critical controls. For most pilots, this level of damage would have been overwhelming, but de Crespigny and his crew stayed calm and took control of the situation.

How He Mastered Crisis Leadership

1. He Focused on Facts, Not Fear.

When the engine exploded, alarms flooded the cockpit. The computer generated over 100 system failure warnings, making it impossible to address everything at once. Instead of panicking, de Crespigny prioritized the most critical failures, focusing on what was still working instead of what was broken.

"We don't crash because of what we don't have. We crash because of what we do with what we have left." – Captain Richard de Crespigny

2. He Kept His Crew Aligned and Empowered.

De Crespigny assigned specific roles to his co-pilots, trusting them to handle key tasks while he focused on navigating the aircraft. By maintaining open communication and delegating effectively, he ensured that every crew member was focused, confident, and engaged in problem-solving. A strong leader doesn't just take control; they empower their team to perform at their best.

3. He Made Decisive, Calculated Choices.

With the aircraft heavily damaged and the possibility of an emergency landing becoming inevitable, de Crespigny ran through multiple scenarios. Instead of rushing a landing, he took extra time to ensure all remaining flight systems were stable. This decision gave the crew time to prepare passengers and emergency personnel on the ground, increasing the chances of a safe landing.

When they finally touched down in Singapore, the brakes overheated, fuel leaked, and a fire risk remained, but every passenger survived.

The Power of Clear Thinking in Crisis

Captain Richard de Crespigny's leadership during Qantas Flight 32's near-disaster is a masterclass in staying calm under extreme pressure. By focusing on facts, leading his team effectively, and making calculated decisions, he prevented panic, stabilized the situation, and ensured a safe landing, turning what could have been a tragedy into an extraordinary example of crisis leadership done right.[194]

Final Leadership Principle: Calm is Contagious

In times of crisis, your actions, demeanor, and decisions will set the tone for everyone around you. Your ability to remain calm under pressure not only helps you make sound decisions; it influences your team to do the same. When you stay composed, others will follow your lead.

Leaders who can maintain calmness, take decisive actions, and communicate transparently will be the ones who not only survive crises but also lead their teams through them with resilience.

Your Action Steps For Today:

- Start working on your "Crisis Playbook."

- Reflect on a past crisis you have experienced: What did you do well, and what could you improve next time?

REMEMBER, CRISES DON'T MAKE LEADERS; THEY REVEAL THEM. HOW YOU RESPOND, COMMUNICATE, AND LEAD DURING TOUGH TIMES WILL DEFINE YOUR LEGACY AS A LEADER.

DAY 27: MASTERING DIFFICULT CONVERSATIONS-HOW TO HANDLE TOUGH TALKS WITH GRACE

TOOLS AND TECHNIQUES TO NAVIGATE THE CONVERSATIONS THAT MATTER MOST

As a leader, you don't get to choose when challenges arise, but you do choose how you respond when tough conversations are needed. Difficult conversations are an unavoidable part of leadership. And yet, many leaders shy away from these uncomfortable discussions, hoping they'll resolve themselves or that someone else will step in. While avoiding tough conversations might seem easier in the short term, it can lead to miscommunication, resentment, and missed opportunities for growth.

"The way you handle tough conversations defines the culture of your team. Great leaders don't avoid hard talks; they navigate them with skill, empathy, and authenticity." – Brene Brown[195]

The 3 C's of Difficult Conversations

The book *Effective Public Relations* by Scott M. Cutlip and Allen H. Center outlines seven C's of effective communication, but we will focus on three today: **Clarity**, **Courtesy**, and **Conciseness**[196]. These principles act as a framework for handling delicate issues while maintaining professionalism and empathy.

1. Clarity: Start with Clear Intentions

Before diving into any tough conversation, it's essential to be crystal clear about your intentions. Are you meeting with the person to correct behavior, resolve a conflict, address a misunderstanding, or simply offer constructive feedback? Without clarity of purpose, your message can become muddled or misinterpreted, leading to unnecessary tension or confusion. As a leader, you should have a clear idea of what you want to achieve and how you want the person to feel during and after the conversation. This clarity helps guide you through the conversation with purpose.

For example, if you need to give feedback on an employee's performance, it's important to clarify the goal of the conversation: Is it to motivate improvement? Is it to identify areas of growth? Or is it to set new expectations? Understanding the objective allows you to communicate in a way that is both purposeful and constructive. The person should know why they are there from the beginning.

2. Courtesy: Practice the Golden Rule

Never forget the human side of the person on the other side of the table. Treat them how you would want to be treated if you were on the receiving end of a difficult conversation. Compassion is the cornerstone of any successful, tough conversation. Without it, a conversation may feel transactional, harsh, or disconnected. When you approach a difficult conversation with genuine empathy and understanding, you invite collaboration rather than confrontation.

Showing courtesy means listening actively and validating the other person's feelings, even when you disagree. It also means acknowledging the difficulty of the conversation and giving the other person space to process and respond. Don't just focus on getting your message across; focus on understanding the other person's perspective and emotions.

For example, imagine giving feedback to an employee who has been missing deadlines. Rather than launching into a list of complaints, you could start by acknowledging the stress they may be facing. You might say, *"I know you've been juggling a lot lately, and I can see you're doing your best. However, I've noticed some deadlines slipping, and I'd like to understand how we can address this together."* By opening the conversation with compassion, you invite a productive and empathetic dialogue.

3. Conciseness: Maintain Control of the Conversation

When emotions run high, it's easy to lose control of a difficult conversation. Conversations can quickly go in a different direction if you are not concise with your message. You must communicate concisely and be able to navigate the conversation back to the focus. You must also be the steady hand guiding the conversation toward resolution. This is not a dominance of control but rather your ability to stay calm and focused and move the conversation toward a positive outcome, no matter how uncomfortable it may be.

Turning Confrontation into Collaboration: The "Mirror & Label" Technique

One powerful technique for diffusing tension and turning confrontation into collaboration is the **"Mirror & Label"** technique[197]. This technique, developed by negotiation expert Chris Voss, involves two key steps:

1. **Mirror**: Repeat what the other person has said, especially if they've expressed strong emotions. This simple act helps to validate their feelings and encourages them to continue talking.

2. **Label**: Name the emotion you believe they are feeling. For example, you might say, *"It sounds like you're frustrated because you didn't feel supported during the last project,"* or *"It seems like you're feeling overwhelmed by the workload."*

By mirroring and labeling, you are acknowledging the other person's experience without judgment. This approach encourages empathy, defuses potential defensiveness, and helps foster a mutual understanding.

Here's how it might play out in a conversation:

- You: *"I noticed that you were upset during the meeting. Could you share more about what's on your mind?"*

- Employee: *"I felt like my ideas were ignored, and that was frustrating. It's happened before."*

- You (Mirror): *"It sounds like you're feeling overlooked."*

- You (Label): *"That must be really frustrating for you."*

You may think (because I do) that this format seems a little awkward, and the person will see straight through what you are doing, and you are right, but the person also values that you understand where they are coming from.

This powerful technique helps create a space where the other person feels heard and validated, making it easier to find a solution together.

Exercise: Preparing for a Difficult Conversation

Preparation is key when it comes to difficult conversations. The steps below can help you prepare for a difficult conversation:

1. **Identify the Issue**: What needs to be addressed or discussed? Be specific about the behavior or situation.

2. **Clarify Your Intentions**: What is the desired outcome of the conversation? When the person walks away from the conversation, what do you hope is accomplished?

3. **Consider Their Perspective**: Think about how the other person might feel about the situation. What emotions might they be experiencing? What points may they argue or become defensive about?

4. **Plan Your Approach**: Before the meeting, script how you will approach the conversation. Keep in mind the 3 C's (Clarity, Courtesy, Conciseness) and use the "Mirror & Label" technique to guide your interaction.

5. **Visualize the Conversation**: Spend a few minutes visualizing the conversation. Picture yourself staying calm and focused, and imagine the conversation unfolding productively.

Leadership Tip: You can also practice the flow of conversation with a trusted colleague. The other person can help you see unclear areas and anticipate questions or objections you may encounter during the conversation. I have done this several times over the years, and I can promise you it is helpful.

The goal of a tough conversation isn't to win, it's to understand, grow, and lead forward. Speak with honesty, lead with heart, and the results will follow.

Case Study: Walt Disney and Tough Creative Decisions

In the 1930s, Walt Disney had an ambitious vision: to create the world's first full-length animated feature film, *Snow White and the Seven Dwarfs*. At the time, the idea of a feature-length cartoon was considered absurd, and many in the industry even referred to the project as "Disney's Folly."

To make this dream a reality, Disney had to convince investors, animators, and his leadership team that the project was worth pursuing despite the financial risks. These conversations were difficult because skepticism and fear of failure loomed over the company.

How Disney Handled Tough Conversations

- **He Acknowledged Concerns but Stood by His Vision:** Disney's leadership team and investors were reluctant to support the film because they feared audiences wouldn't sit through an 80-minute animated film. Instead of dismissing their concerns, Disney listened carefully and addressed each of their doubts with a combination of data, storytelling, and unwavering belief in the project.

- **He Used a Collaborative Approach:** Disney encouraged open dialogue with his animators and executives. He gathered feedback, adjusted details, and ensured everyone felt part of the creative process. This approach prevented unnecessary conflict and helped the team feel invested in the vision rather than forced into it.

- **He Balanced Empathy with Decisiveness:** Disney remained focused on his dream despite financial and creative pushback. He knew that not everyone would agree, but standing firm in a well-thought-out decision was key.

"It's kind of fun to do the impossible." – Walt Disney

The Outcome: When *Snow White and the Seven Dwarfs* was released in 1937, it became a massive success, proving that animated feature films could captivate audiences worldwide. Disney's ability to navigate difficult conversations transformed doubt into innovation, leading to one of the most influential entertainment empires of all time.[198]

The Power of Mastering Tough Talks

Walt Disney's story reminds us that leaders must embrace difficult conversations as opportunities for growth. By balancing vision, empathy, and decisiveness, tough discussions can lead to breakthrough moments, not just for leaders but for entire organizations.

Final Leadership Principle: Embrace the Tough Conversations

As a leader, the **most impactful conversations are often the hardest ones**. Mastering tough conversations is an essential skill that every effective leader must have. Difficult conversations are essential to build deeper connections, collaboration, and positive change among those you lead.

Your Action Steps For Today:

1. **Prepare for an upcoming difficult conversation** using the steps outlined above.

2. **Practice the "Mirror & Label" technique** to empathize with the other person's perspective.

YOU WON'T ALWAYS GET IT PERFECT, BUT WHEN YOU SHOW UP WITH INTENTION, EMPATHY, AND CLARITY, YOUR LEADERSHIP WILL LEAVE A LASTING IMPACT, ONE CONVERSATION AT A TIME.

Day 28: The Power of Storytelling-How Leaders Use Stories to Inspire

Turning Experiences into Impact

As a leader, one of your most powerful tools isn't your expertise, strategy, or even your charisma; it's your ability to tell a compelling story. Storytelling has been used for centuries to convey values, influence others, and spark action. What makes leaders memorable is their ability to resonate beyond their accomplishments. They weave stories that inspire, motivate, and build a lasting connection with their audience.

In today's fast-paced world, where attention spans are short and distractions are abundant, cutting through the noise and capturing people's imaginations is more valuable than ever. Facts tell, but stories sell. This holds true in leadership as much as it does in marketing. As a leader, the stories you tell shape your team's culture, influence your organization's direction, and ignite passion in those you lead.

Effective storytelling doesn't require you to be a natural-born storyteller or a gifted public speaker. With the right framework and intention, any leader can harness the power of storytelling to drive results and inspire loyalty.[199]

"Embracing the power of storytelling! I've learned that diving deep into personal stories is not just an option; it's a MUST in any speech." – Keith Ferrazzi[200]

Why Storytelling is the Ultimate Tool for Persuasion and Leadership

In his book *Made to Stick*, Chip Heath and Dan Heath outline why some ideas stick while others don't. One of the main reasons stories resonate is that they **appeal to emotion and logic**. While facts, figures, and data provide information, they often fail to engage the audience at an emotional level. In contrast, stories activate the emotional centers of the brain, allowing listeners to feel what the storyteller is conveying. This emotional connection makes people listen and care about what's being said.[201]

As a leader, storytelling allows you to:

1. Simplify Complex Ideas: A well-crafted story can make complex concepts understandable and relatable.

2. Engage Emotionally: Stories create an emotional connection that data and facts alone cannot.

3. Inspire Action: By connecting values, challenges, and triumphs through storytelling, you motivate people to act in ways that align with your vision.

4. Create a Shared Vision: Stories help convey the values and purpose that bind a group together, creating alignment and a sense of community within your team.

One powerful reason why storytelling works in leadership is because stories naturally build trust. When leaders share their own personal experiences, failures, and triumphs, they allow others to see them as human; someone who has walked the same path as their team members and faced similar challenges.

This vulnerability creates an authentic connection and makes leaders more relatable.

The 3-Part Storytelling Framework That Makes People Take Action

Effective leaders don't just tell stories for the sake of storytelling; they tell stories with intention and purpose. Every story you tell should align with a clear objective. Whether you're trying to motivate, inspire, or persuade, you can use a simple, **3-part framework** to structure your stories and make them impactful. This framework is based on **The Hero's Journey**, a narrative model used in countless stories across cultures and history. It has 3 phases; each phase has many steps. There are a total of 12 steps.

1. Departure: Set Up the Problem

Every great story begins with a challenge or conflict, something that needs to be overcome. The first part of your leadership story should set the scene, outlining the problem you are facing. This could be a personal struggle, a business obstacle, or a challenge faced by your team. The key is to present it in a way that makes your audience relate to the struggle.

The struggle sets the foundation of your story, it draws the audience in and allows them to connect with what you are experiencing. It paints a picture of the tension or conflict that needs resolution.

2. Initiation: The Transformation

After introducing the struggle, the next part of your story is the transformation; the pivotal turning point where change begins to happen. This is where the lessons, decisions, and actions taken lead to positive outcomes. This phase shows growth and overcoming adversity, and it's where the audience sees that despite the obstacles, progress was made.

This is also the part of the story where you, as a leader, should highlight your decision-making process. What choices did you make that led to success? What lessons did you learn along the way? How did your team respond to the changes?

The transformation is the heart of the story, showing the lessons learned and the impact of those lessons on the team or organization. It's where your leadership is most evident.

3. Return: The Resolution

Every great story ends with a resolution, the positive outcome that results from the actions taken. This is where you show how the problem was solved, the team grew, and the goals were achieved. In a leadership story, the resolution is the result of your efforts and the efforts of your team.

The resolution should relate to your core message. What did you want to achieve by telling this story? What action do you want your listeners to take? The resolution should inspire your audience to believe they can overcome the obstacle or achieve success as well.[202]

Exercise: Write a 1-Minute Story

It's your turn to craft a story. Think about a time when you overcame something or learned a lesson that could inspire others. Now, use the 3-part framework to craft your story:

1. The Struggle: What challenge or problem did you face? What emotions did you feel? What situation initiated the problem?

2. The Transformation: What decisions or actions did you take to overcome it, and how? Share how you felt in those moments. Share what you did.

3. The Resolution: What was the outcome? What lesson was learned?

Once you've written your story, share it with a colleague or team member. See if they resonate with your message. Does it inspire them to act? Does it communicate the value you intended?

Case Study: Dame Anita Roddick – Building a Brand Through Storytelling and Social Activism

Dame Anita Roddick, the founder of *The Body Shop*, is one of the most remarkable examples of using storytelling to build a business with a purpose. From the beginning, Roddick understood the power of storytelling in creating an emotional connection with customers. She didn't just sell beauty products; she sold a story.

Roddick's storytelling wasn't limited to advertising; she wove the company's values into every aspect of its operations. For example, The Body Shop's campaigns weren't just about selling cosmetics; they were about fighting animal testing, empowering women, and promoting environmental sustainability. Roddick's personal commitment to these causes became a core part of the brand's identity. She used storytelling to not only sell products but also to share a larger message about making the world a better place.

As a result, The Body Shop became a global brand with a loyal customer base who believed in the company's mission. Roddick's ability to weave stories of activism into her business model created deep emotional connections with customers and employees alike. The power of her storytelling lies in the fact that it was authentic, purpose-driven, and aligned with the company's values.[203]

"Storytelling is the most powerful way to put ideas into the world today." – *Robert McKee*[204]

Final Leadership Principle: Master Storytelling, Master Influence

In leadership, the stories you tell define the culture you create, the values you uphold, and the impact you have on others. When you **master the art of storytelling**, you harness the power to influence, inspire, and lead with purpose. Whether you're giving feedback, motivating your team, or sharing your vision for the future, stories have the ability to create emotional connections and drive action.

Your Action Steps For Today:

- **Identify a core value** you want to instill in your team and think of a way to weave it into a story that will inspire action.

- Using the core value identified above, **craft a leadership story** using the 3-part storytelling framework. Share it with someone on your team and ask for feedback.

STORYTELLING ISN'T JUST ABOUT TELLING A GOOD STORY-IT'S ABOUT CREATING A LEGACY OF INFLUENCE THAT SHAPES THE FUTURE OF YOUR LEADERSHIP AND YOUR ORGANIZATION.

DAY 29: BUILDING A LEADERSHIP LEGACY-WHAT WILL YOU LEAVE BEHIND?

WHAT YOU BUILD IN OTHERS WILL OUTLAST ANYTHING YOU BUILD ALONE

Leadership is often viewed through the lens of authority, titles, or achievements; how many promotions someone has had, how many accolades they've earned, or how much success they've cultivated within an organization. However, true leadership, the kind that endures and continues to inspire long after the leader has stepped away, isn't about titles or personal accolades. It's about the impact you have on others, the lives you touch, and the legacy you leave behind.

When you think of great leaders, those whose influence has withstood the test of time, what stands out? Is it their titles? Their ability to grow businesses? Or is it the way they empowered others, the way they inspired change, the way they made people feel seen and heard? Most likely, it's the latter.

Leadership isn't measured by how much recognition you receive but by the positive impact you create in the lives of others. Every leader should ask themselves: *What kind of legacy do I want to leave?*

The mark of a true leader isn't found in their achievements alone; it's found in how their work lives on through the people they've empowered and the changes they've initiated.

The "Impact Audit" – Assessing How Your Leadership Affects Others

Before you can build a leadership legacy, it's important to understand where you currently stand. The first step in this process is conducting an **Impact Audit,** a personal reflection on how your leadership currently affects others. You must be honest with yourself: Are you creating an environment that fosters growth, trust, and empowerment? Or are you inadvertently stifling others, focusing too much on the short-term, and not providing the kind of support that truly helps people thrive?

The **Impact Audit**[205] requires you to assess your leadership in multiple dimensions:

- **The People You Lead:** Think about how your leadership affects the individuals within your team. Do they feel supported, encouraged, and empowered to do their best work? Are you giving them the space to grow and develop, or are you holding them back with micromanagement or a lack of trust? Leadership is about service, not control. Great leaders help others reach their full potential.

- **Your Team's Culture:** What kind of culture have you created within your team or organization? Is it one that encourages collaboration, transparency, and open communication, or does it foster fear, competition, and disengagement? The culture you build speaks volumes about the kind of leader you are and the legacy you'll leave behind.

- **Your Long-Term Impact:** Think beyond your immediate circle. What is the lasting impact of your leadership on your community, your industry, or the world? Leadership is not just about results in the short term; it's about creating change that has lasting effects.

After you reflect on these questions, consider the areas where you can improve. A leadership legacy is not just about what you do right; it's about continually striving to make a positive impact. Regular audits like this will help you stay focused on the things that matter most: people, culture, and long-term influence.

The 4 Key Components of a Lasting Leadership Legacy

Now that you've reflected on your current impact, it's time to think about what makes up a leadership legacy. A truly lasting legacy is built on four key components:

1. **Values-Driven Leadership:** The foundation of any strong leadership legacy is rooted in values. Your core values as a leader will shape your behavior, decisions, and interactions with others. Integrity, honesty, and compassion are just a few of the values that define great leaders. When people think about your legacy, they should immediately associate it with the values you held dear and how those values shaped the way you led.

2. **Empowering Others:** True leaders don't just accomplish things for themselves; they empower others to do the same. A lasting legacy enables others to lead and succeed in their own right. When you invest in developing others, whether by mentoring, providing opportunities,

or fostering an environment of growth, you're laying the foundation for a legacy that extends far beyond your career.

3. **Creating a Lasting Impact:** A leadership legacy is about more than just building a successful team or achieving personal success; it's about creating an enduring impact on the world. This could be through the products or services your company makes, the causes you champion, or the ways you challenge the status quo. Leadership is about creating something that lasts and will benefit future generations.

4. **Leaving a Positive Cultural Footprint:** The culture you cultivate directly reflects your leadership. When people think of your leadership legacy, they should think of the values, principles, and norms you established and how they influenced the people around you. Your leadership legacy is often carried forward by the culture you leave behind, one that persists even when you're no longer in charge.[206]

Exercise: Write Your Leadership Legacy Statement

Now that you've had time to reflect on what constitutes a leadership legacy, it's time to craft your own leadership legacy statement. This is a personal declaration of the impact you hope to have in the next 5, 10, or even 20 years. What do you want to be remembered for? What will your team, your organization, or your community say about the way you led?

Take a few minutes to reflect on the following questions:

1. What values do I want to embody as a leader?

2. How do I want to empower others through my

leadership?

3. What kind of impact do I want to create in the world?

4. What kind of culture do I want to leave behind?

Now, write a short (1-2 paragraph) leadership legacy statement that reflects your answers to these questions. This statement will serve as a guiding light for the rest of your leadership journey, helping you stay focused on the impact you want to create.

Case Study: Fred Rogers - Building a Leadership Legacy Based on Kindness and Authenticity

Fred Rogers, the creator and host of *Mister Rogers' Neighborhood*, built one of the most enduring leadership legacies through his unique approach to children's television. His legacy is based not on accolades or commercial success but on the values he imposed: kindness, empathy, and authenticity.

Rogers understood that the true power of leadership lies not in impressing others with grand accomplishments but in creating a sense of safety and belonging. He treated each viewer as if they were a friend, addressing them directly and encouraging them to be their true selves. His leadership legacy continues today, not just through his television show but through the countless leaders he inspired to be kind, genuine, and authentic in their own right.[207]

Fred Rogers didn't just change television; he changed the way people lead, showing us that kindness is the most powerful leadership tool.

Final Leadership Principle: Your Legacy Is Your True Measure of Leadership

Leadership is not defined by the title you hold or the achievements you make. The true measure of your leadership is the impact you have on the lives of others and the legacy you leave behind. As you continue your leadership journey, ask yourself: What kind of leader do I want to be?

Your leadership legacy is shaped by the choices you make today. Choose to lead with intention, to empower others, and to create a positive impact that will resonate long after you're gone.

Your Action Steps For Today:

- **Write your Leadership Legacy Statement**. Reflect on the impact you want to have in the next 10 years and craft a statement that captures that vision.

- **Take the Impact Audit**. Assess how your leadership currently affects others and identify areas where you can create a more lasting, positive impact.

LEADERSHIP IS ABOUT MORE THAN JUST ACHIEVING RESULTS; IT'S ABOUT CREATING A LEGACY OF INFLUENCE, EMPOWERMENT, AND POSITIVE CHANGE. WHAT WILL YOUR LEGACY BE?

DAY 30: THE LEADERSHIP CHALLENGE NEVER ENDS-YOUR NEXT STEPS

THIS ISN'T THE FINISH LINE...IT'S THE STARTING POINT

Leadership is a dynamic, ever-evolving journey, not a one-time achievement. It's not a position you attain and then rest upon; instead, it's an ongoing process of growth, learning, and adapting. Over the past 29 days, you've cultivated habits and mindsets that will be the foundation of your leadership journey. But as you stand at the end of this initial challenge in your leadership growth, the most crucial question is: **What happens next?**

Leadership isn't a 30-day challenge with a clear finish line. In fact, **leadership is never really "finished"**. As soon as you think you've mastered one area, a new challenge presents itself. The world around you constantly changes; new technologies emerge, new leaders rise, and the needs of your team and organization evolve.

The real measure of leadership is not just what you do today but how you adapt, grow, and remain relevant for tomorrow.

Your leadership journey doesn't end today. Instead, this is just the beginning. The habits and principles you've developed over the past month are only the starting point for what you can continue to build.

"Leadership is not a position or a title; it is action and example."
– Cory Booker[208]

Leadership is a Journey, Not a Destination

Too often, we approach leadership as a checklist: *"I'll read these books, attend these seminars, and then I'll be a great leader."* But leadership is much more complex than that. Great leaders don't stop learning once they reach a certain point; they understand that leadership is a journey that requires continuous learning and change.

Every step you take as a leader should be fueled by curiosity, a desire to improve, and a willingness to challenge your thinking. Leadership isn't about reaching a finish line; it's about navigating an evolving landscape. As you progress in your leadership journey, there will always be new things to learn, new people to lead, and new challenges to overcome.

The Growth Loop: Learn-Apply-Reflect-Adjust-Repeat

Now that you've completed the 30-day leadership challenge, it's time to turn the next phase of your development into an ongoing process. This is where the *Growth Loop*[209] comes in. The *Growth*

Loop is a simple yet powerful cycle that can guide your leadership development for years to come.

1. **Learn**: The first step in the loop is to continue your learning process. Whether it's through reading books, attending seminars, talking to mentors, or observing other leaders, always make space for learning. The world is constantly evolving, and so should you. Keep your learning continuous and diverse.

2. **Apply**: The next step is to put your knowledge into practice. Leadership isn't just about theory; it's about action. Apply what you've learned in real-world situations. Whether you're making decisions, leading a team, or tackling a challenging problem, the application phase is where the magic happens.

3. **Reflect:** Once you've applied your learning, step back and reflect on how things went. What worked well? What didn't? What could you do differently next time? Reflection is essential for growth. It allows you to process and learn from your experiences, ensures you don't repeat the same mistakes, and allows you to build upon your successes.

4. **Adjust**: Based on your reflection, adjust your approach. If something didn't go as planned, modify your strategy. If something worked well, figure out how to do more of it. Adjustment is about being flexible and ensuring you continue growing and improving. Adapt your tactics, strategies, and mindset as necessary.

5. **Repeat**: The final step is to repeat the loop. Learning, applying, reflecting, and adjusting should be an ongoing cycle. Over time, this loop will help you refine your leadership style and approach. It will also help you build

resilience as you learn to adapt and grow through every challenge you face.

Exercise: Set Your Next 90-Day Leadership Challenge

Leadership growth doesn't stop when the 30 days are over. In fact, it's just beginning. As a leader, it's essential to set concrete, actionable goals for yourself that will keep you moving forward. **What will you focus on in the next 90 days?**

Here's how to get started:

1. **Identify a Specific Leadership Skill to Improve**: Maybe you want to improve your communication skills, your ability to delegate, or your emotional intelligence. Whatever it is, identify a key leadership area that you want to improve. This will be the focus of your 90-day challenge.[210]

2. **Set Measurable Goals**: Define what success looks like. For example, if your goal is to improve communication, you might aim to give a certain number of public presentations, lead more team meetings, or engage in active listening with your team. Make your goals specific and measurable.[211]

3. **Create a Plan**: Develop a strategy for how you will achieve these goals. Break down each goal into smaller, manageable tasks. Set deadlines and milestones to ensure you stay on track.[212]

4. **Commit to Accountability**: Share your 90-day challenge with a mentor, coach, or trusted colleague who can help hold you accountable. Regular check-ins will help keep you motivated and ensure that you're making

progress.[213]

5. **Review and Reflect**: After the 90 days, review your progress. Did you achieve your goals? What worked well, and what could you improve upon? Use your reflections to start a new growth cycle and continue developing as a leader.[214]

Case Study: How Arianna Huffington Continues to Evolve as a Leader

Remember Arianna Huffington from Day 25? Let's see how she took the next steps in her leadership after extreme burnout. She was the founder of the Huffington Post and has always been a leader who exemplifies the importance of continuous learning and growth. After stepping down as CEO of her company, Huffington faced a new set of challenges: how to evolve as a leader while transitioning into a new career phase. Huffington embraced the opportunity to learn and grow in new ways. She launched **Thrive Global**, a company focused on improving well-being and helping people avoid burnout.[215]

Huffington's story is a perfect example of how leadership is an ongoing journey. She didn't stop growing after her initial success; she recognized that personal and professional development never ends, no matter how accomplished you become. She adapted to new challenges, embraced new opportunities, and continually refined her leadership style.

"Success is not about climbing the ladder of success; it's about expanding the ladder so everyone can climb it." – Arianna Huffington[216]

Final Leadership Principle: Keep the Growth Loop Going

You've completed the 30-day leadership challenge. Congratulations! But this is just the beginning of your leadership journey. **The true test of leadership is not in a one-time effort but in your ongoing commitment to growth, learning, and adaptation.** The Growth Loop: Learn, Apply, Reflect, Adjust, Repeat, will keep you on the path toward continuous improvement.

As you move forward in your leadership journey, remember this: **The leadership challenge never ends.**

Your Action Steps For Today:

1. **Set your next 90-day leadership challenge**. Identify one leadership skill you want to improve and create a concrete plan to work on it.

2. **Commit to the Growth Loop**. Make learning, applying, reflecting, and adjusting part of your regular routine as you continue to grow as a leader.

STAY CURIOUS, STAY COMMITTED, AND KEEP GROWING. LEADERSHIP IS A JOURNEY THAT NEVER STOPS. WHAT'S YOUR NEXT STEP?

Thank you for joining me on this journey. If this book has encouraged or inspired you, I'd be so grateful if you'd take a moment to leave a review. Your words not only mean a lot to me but also help other leaders discover the tools they need to grow.

Michelle

Your Leadership Journey Continues

Congratulations! You've made it to the end of your 30-day leadership challenge! How did it go? You have had thirty days of learning, stretching, and growing. Never forget that leadership is not a program with a finish line. It's not a title you attain or a box you check off. Leadership is a journey, an evolving practice that calls for your presence, your courage, and your willingness to show up every single day.

The fact that you're reading these words means that something inside of you is drawn to the idea of making a lasting impact. You are not content to simply go through the motions. You want to lead with purpose. You want to influence and inspire. Most importantly, you want to **keep going.**

The best leaders of our time often stumble. Even the most inspiring figures have moments of doubt, exhaustion, and frustration. The difference between those who lead with impact and those who fade into the background is simple: **resilience and commitment to the journey.**

If you remember nothing else from this book, remember this: **leadership is a lifelong journey.** You will never have all the answers. You will never reach the final stage of perfection. But if you remain committed to learning, adapting, and leading with authenticity, you will leave a lasting imprint on the world around you.

The Heart of Leadership: It's About Others

Throughout this journey, you've learned strategies, read case studies, and practiced new ways of thinking. But at its core, leadership is not about tactics. **Leadership is about people.** It's about how you show up for those you lead, how you invest in their growth, and how you make them feel.

So, as you step forward from these 30 days, ask yourself:

- How can I uplift and empower those around me?

- How can I be a leader who listens more than I speak?

- How can I create opportunities for others to shine?

When you commit to lifting others up, your leadership legacy takes shape, not through words, but through action. **The greatest leaders don't build followers; they build more leaders.**

Leadership as a Daily Practice

By now, you know that leadership isn't something you do once; it's something you practice daily. Growth is not an event; it's a **way of being.** The truth is you won't always feel motivated. You won't always feel like making the extra effort. But **discipline beats motivation every time.**

Know this: You will face obstacles, have moments of frustration, and question whether the work you're doing is making an impact.

But when you adopt a **growth mindset**, you begin to see every challenge as an opportunity.

"Success is not final, failure is not fatal: it is the courage to continue that counts." – Winston Churchill

So when setbacks arise, when uncertainty clouds your vision, remind yourself: **This is part of the journey.**

Ending with Where We Started: Never Forget Your Why

One of the most important leadership lessons is this: Never forget why you do what you do. Your why is your driving force; without a why, you will simply be going through the motions and will burn out easily.

"People don't buy WHAT you do, they buy WHY you do it." - Simon Sinek

Stay True to Your Core Values

Ask yourself:

- What values define me as a leader?

- What are the non-negotiables I will never compromise?

- Am I leading in a way that aligns with my deepest beliefs?

A leader who is clear on their values creates trust. And trust is the currency of leadership. **People will follow you not because of what you do but because of who you are.**

The Final Challenge: Your Next Bold Step

So here you are, standing at the edge of everything you've learned over the past 30 days. And now, the question is: **What will you do next?**

You could close this book and move on, carrying a few good insights but making no real change. **Or you could take action.**

Here's your final challenge: **Make a leadership commitment that will push you forward.** Right now, decide on one bold action you will take in the next 30 days. Not someday. Not eventually. **Now.**

Here are a few ideas to get you started:

- Step into a leadership role you've been avoiding.

- Have a tough conversation you've been putting off.

- Start mentoring someone who needs your guidance.

- Launch a new initiative that excites and challenges you.

- Commit to learning something that will expand your leadership abilities.

"The best way to predict the future is to create it." – Peter Drucker

Whatever it is, make sure it stretches you. **Growth doesn't happen in your comfort zone.** True leadership begins when you step into the unknown with courage and conviction.

Final Words: The Leader Within You

You don't need permission to lead. You don't need a title to make an impact. You already have everything you need to lead with influence, authenticity, and purpose. **Leadership is not about**

waiting for the right moment; it's about stepping up right now.

The world needs leaders who are bold, who are kind, who are willing to take risks, and push boundaries for the greater good. The world needs **you.**

So, take what you've learned. Carry it forward. Continue growing. Continue leading.

Now go lead.

ACKNOWLEDGEMENTS

I want to express my deepest gratitude to all who have supported me on my leadership and book-writing journey. I would not be where I am today without the countless individuals who have encouraged me along the way.

Thank you, Bruce Marchand, for giving me my first teaching job and instilling in me the belief that I have what it takes to be a leader.

Thank you, Marlo Keller, for trusting me and investing in my growth during my first leadership position. You taught me the importance of leading with intentionality and modeled a relentless dedication to serving others.

Thank you, Kathy Behrendsen, for being my ride-or-die partner in crime. You pushed me in so many ways and helped me learn not to take things too seriously, focusing instead on what truly matters. I could not have succeeded in my first few years as a principal without you!

To all the amazing staff members at EA Lawhon Elementary and Roy J. Wollam Elementary, thank you for embarking on this journey with me and making my job easy and fulfilling. I could not have asked for a better group of people to lead.

Thank you to Jenni, Lisa, and Leah for supporting me during my new leadership journey this past year. Your encouragement as I took on this new adventure is something I will always treasure.

Thank you to Shannon and Meredith for the countless hours reading over the book, editing it, and providing suggestions on how to enhance its flow and clarity.

Last but not least, thank you to Chelsea for always encouraging me, to Brad for helping me with over 100 tech questions and serving as a sounding board for creative ideas, and to Chad for being with me on this long journey of becoming a leader. You have always provided me the space and time to grow and have been my biggest supporter.

"FOR I KNOW THE PLANS I HAVE FOR YOU, PLANS TO PROSPER YOU AND NOT TO HARM YOU, PLANS TO GIVE YOU HOPE AND A FUTURE." -JEREMIAH 29:11

ABOUT THE AUTHOR

Michelle Pourchot is a seasoned educational leader with over 29 years in education and 20 years of experience as an elementary school principal. Known for cultivating positive school cultures and developing strong teams, Michelle has spent her career helping others grow, thrive, and lead with purpose.

Michelle has been married to her high school sweetheart for over 30 years. Together, they've raised two incredible adult children and are now proud grandparents to three energetic and adorable grandchildren. She shares her home with two loyal dogs and enjoys spending time outdoors. From camping under the stars to relaxing on a cruise ship deck, she understands the importance of balancing leadership with life.

Michelle's greatest passion is empowering people. Whether mentoring educators, speaking on leadership, or writing books like this one, her mission remains to inspire others to learn, lead boldly, and reach their full potential; one intentional day at a time.

ENDNOTES

1. Maxwell, J. (1998). *The 21 Irrefutable Laws of Leadership* (p. 86). Thomas Nelson.

2. Find Your WHY and Find More Profits | Inspire Results Business Coaching. https://inspireresults.com/findyouwhyandfind-more-profits/

3. Sinek, S., 2009, Start With You Why, TED Conferences, retrieved from https://www.youtube.com/watch?v=u4ZoJKF_VuA

4. Becoming a Leader Is Synonymous With Becoming Yourself. It Is Precisely That Simple, and It Is Also That Difficult.. https://www.starfirecodes.com/p/becoming-a-leader-is-synonymous-with

5. Dweck, C. S. (2006). *Mindset: The new psychology of success.* Random House.

6. Maxwell, J. C. (2012). *The 15 invaluable laws of growth: Live them and reach your potential.* Center Street.

7. Dweck, C. S. (2006). *Mindset: The new psychology of success.* Random House.

8. Eurich, T. (2018, October 17). Working with people who aren't self-aware. *Harvard Business Review.*https://hbr.org/2018/10/working-with-people-who-arent-self-aware

9. Drucker, P. F. (2005). *Manage yourself and then your company: Set an example.* IEDC-Bled School of Management.

10. Eurich, T. (2018, October 17). Working with people who aren't self-aware. *Harvard Business Review.* https://hbr.org/2018/10/working-with-people-who-a rent-self-aware

11. Gribble, N., Ladyshewsky, R. K., & Parsons, R. (2018). Changes in the emotional intelligence of occupational therapy students during practice education: A longitudinal study. British Journal of Occupational Therapy. https://doi.org/10.1177/0308022618763501

12. Goleman, D. (1995). *Emotional intelligence: Why it can matter more than IQ.* Bantam Books.

13. (2016). Sound Bites. Journal of Property Management, 81(1), 4.

14. The Vital Role of Leadership Training for First-Time Managers – Arden Executive Coaching. https://ardencoaching.com/leadership-training-for-first-tim e-managers/

15. TalentSmart. (n.d.). *Better EQ, better performance.* Retrieved March 24, 2025, from https://www.talentsmarteq.com/emotional-intelligence-at-workplace-to-improve-performance/

16. Gallup. (2021). *Employee retention and burnout: Trends and strategies for 2025.* Retrieved March 24, 2025, from https://b2bdaily.com/hrtech/employee-retention-and-burn out-trends-and-strategies-for-2025/

17. Leadership Training Courses | 3 Pillars of Leaders. https://www.3pillarsofleadership.com/solutions/leadership -training-courses

18. Workplace Innovation. (n.d.). *Emotionally intelligent leadership*. Retrieved March 24, 2025, from https://workplaceinnovation.eu/wp-content/uploads/2022/ 07/Emotionally-Intelligent-Leadership.pdf

19. Mindful Wagering for Mental Health: Responsible Strategies - Curious Mind Magazine. https://curiousmindmagazine.com/mindful-wagering-for-m ental-health-responsible-strategies/

20. Unlocking Success: The Power of Emotional Intelligence Leadership. https://essemy.com.au/ei-in-leadership-why-it-is-crucial-for -success/

21. Mastering the Modern World: [5 Critical Skills for Thriving in Today's Complex Landscape]. https://www.thatlovepodcast.com/post/mastering-the-mod ern-world-5-critical-skills-for-thriving-in-today-s-complex-la ndscape

22. Google. (n.d.). *re:Work - Managers*. Retrieved March 24, 2025, from https://rework.withgoogle.com/en/subjects/managers

23. Sinek, S. (2016). *Together is better: A little book of inspiration*. Portfolio/Penguin

24. Ford, H. (n.d.). *Whether you think you can, or you think you can't—you're right* [Quote]. In Quote Investigator. Retrieved April 14, 2025, from https://quoteinvestigator.com/2010/07/22/can-do/

25. Carney, D. R., Cuddy, A. J. C., & Yap, A. J. (2010). Power posing: Brief nonverbal displays affect neuroendocrine levels and risk tolerance. *Psychological Science, 21*(10), 1363–1368.

26. Cuddy, A. (2012, June). *Your body language shapes who you are* . TED Conferences. https://www.ted.com/talks/amy_cuddy_your_body_languag e_shapes_who_you_are

27. Sinek, S. (2009, September). *How great leaders inspire action.* TED Conferences. https://www.ted.com/talks/simon_sinek_how_great_leaders _inspire_action

28. how to meet people... | Social Anxiety Support Forum. https://www.socialanxietysupport.com/threads/how-to-me et-people.61664/?u=14844

29. Roosevelt, T. (n.d.). *In any moment of decision, the best thing you can do is the right thing, the next best thing is the wrong thing, and the worst thing you can do is nothing* [Quote]. In Quote Investigator. Retrieved April 14, 2025, from https://quoteinvestigator.com/2018/09/01/decision/

30. Bezos, J. (2016). *2016 Letter to Shareholders.* Amazon.com. Retrieved March 27, 2025, from https://www.amazon.com/letter2016

31. Chun, C., & Whitt, J. E. (2019). John Boyd and the "OODA" loop (Great strategists). *War Room – U.S. Army War College.* Retrieved March 27, 2025, from https://warroom.armywarcollege.edu/special-series/great-s trategists/boyd-ooda-loop-great-strategists/

32. Welch, S. (2009). *10-10-10: A fast and powerful way to get unstuck in love, at work, and with your family.* Scribner.

33. Bezos, J. (2015). *2015 Letter to Shareholders*. Amazon.com. Retrieved March 27, 2025, from https://www.amazon.com/letter2015

34. Isaacson, W. (2011). *Steve Jobs*. Simon & Schuster.

35. Mandela, N. (n.d.). "Do not judge me by my successes; judge me by how many times I fell down and got back up again."

36. Cross, R., Dillon, K., & Greenberg, D. (2021). The secret to building resilience. *Harvard Business Review*. Retrieved from https://hbr.org/2021/01/the-secret-to-building-resilience

37. McKinsey & Company. (2020). Building organizational resilience. *McKinsey & Company*. Retrieved from https://www.mckinsey.com/capabilities/people-and-organizational-performance/our-insights/raising-the-resilience-of-your-organization

38. Gallup. (2024). Employee engagement. *Gallup News*. Retrieved from https://news.gallup.com/topic/employee-engagement.aspx

39. Leadership Institute. (2023). *The 3-step resilience framework: Strategies for overcoming adversity.* Leadership Insights. https://www.leadershipinsights.com/resilience-framework

40. Pak, E. (2020, June 17). *Walt Disney's Rocky Road to Success*. Biography. https://www.biography.com/movies-tv/walt-disney-failures

41. Ignatius, A. (2010, July–August). The HBR interview: "We had to own the mistakes." *Harvard Business Review*. https://hbr.org/2010/07/the-hbr-interview-we-had-to-own-the-mistakes

42. Caprino, K. (2012, May 23). *10 lessons I learned from Sara Blakely that you won't hear in business school*. Forbes. https://www.forbes.com/sites/kathycaprino/2012/05/23/10 -lessons-i-learned-from-sara-blakely-that-you-wont-hear-in-business-school

43. Duckworth, A. L., & Peterson, C. (2007). Grit: Perseverance and passion for long-term goals. *Journal of Personality and Social Psychology*, 92(6), 1087–1101. https://doi.org/10.1037/0022-3514.92.6.1087

44. Edmondson, A. C. (2011). Strategies for learning from failure. *Harvard Business Review*, 89(4), 48–55. https://hbr.org/2011/04/strategies-for-learning-from-failure

45. Gallup. (n.d.). State of the American manager: Analytics and advice for leaders. https://www.gallup.com/services/182138/state-american-m anager-report.aspx

46. Rowling, J. K. (2015). *Very good lives: The fringe benefits of failure and the importance of imagination*. Little, Brown and Company.

47. Warren Buffett Quote - The difference between successful .... https://inspirational-quotes.space/quote/the-difference-bet ween-successful-people-and-really-successful-people-is-tha t-really-successful-people-say-no-to-almost-everything/

48. Gates, B. (n.d.). *Personal communication*.

49. Gates, B. (n.d.). *How I manage my time for maximum productivity*. Bill & Melinda Gates Foundation. Retrieved from https://www.gatesfoundation.org

50. Covey, S. R. (1989). *The 7 habits of highly effective people: Powerful lessons in personal change*. Free Press.

51. Leveling Up. (2015). *Why you shouldn't waste your time on $10 per hour tasks*. Leveling Up. https://www.levelingup.com/productivity/why-you-shouldnt-waste-your-time-on-10-per-hour-tasks/

52. Allen, D. (2001). *Getting things done: The art of stress-free productivity*. New York: Viking.

53. Gates, B. (n.d.). *How I manage my time for maximum productivity*. Bill & Melinda Gates Foundation. Retrieved from https://www.gatesfoundation.org

54. Buffett, W. (n.d.). *It takes 20 years to build a reputation and five minutes to ruin it.* [Quote]. Retrieved from https://www.goodreads.com/quotes/20610-it-takes-20-years-to-build-a-reputation-and-five

55. Babson College. (n.d.). *Why is integrity important in leadership?* Babson Thought & Action. Retrieved from https://entrepreneurship.babson.edu/why-is-integrity-important-in-leadership/Investor's Business Daily. (n.d.). *Be authentic by sticking to your principles.* Investor's Business Daily. Retrieved from https://www.investors.com/news/management/leaders-and-success/be-authentic-by-sticking-to-your-principles/

56. Wikipedia contributors. (2023, September 24). Howard Schultz. In *Wikipedia, The Free Encyclopedia*. https://en.wikipedia.org/wiki/Howard_Schultz

57. Ignatius, A. (2010, July–August). We had to own the mistakes: An interview with Howard Schultz. *Harvard Business Review*. https://hbr.org/2010/07/the-hbr-interview-we-had-to-own-the-mistakes

58. Morrison, D. (2013, March 8). *Address at the International Women's Day Conference*. United Nations International Women's Day Conference.

59. Effective Delegation - Effective Managers. https://effectivemanagers.com/consultants/effective-delegation-empowering-teams-for-better-results/

60. Dewey, J. (1938). *Experience and education*. New York, NY: Macmillan.

61. Aurelius, M. (2014). *Meditations* (M. Hammond, Trans.). Penguin Classics.

62. Edutopia. (n.d.). *6 tips for teachers to make reflection a consistent habit*. Retrieved from https://www.edutopia.org/article/consistent-teacher-reflection-tips/

63. ASCD. (n.d.). *5 simple reflection practices*. *Educational Leadership*. Retrieved from https://www.ascd.org/el/mental-health-matters

64. University of Edinburgh. (n.d.). *Reflection toolkit: Goals, objectives, habits*. Retrieved from https://reflection.ed.ac.uk/reflectors-toolkit/goals-objectives-habits

65. British Psychological Society. (n.d.). *Eight routes to a reflective habit*. *The Psychologist*. Retrieved from https://www.bps.org.uk/psychologist/eight-routes-reflective-habit

66. Maxwell, J. C. (2014). *Good leaders ask great questions: Your foundation for successful leadership*. Center Street.

67. Groeschel, C. (n.d.). *How to develop leaders* [Audio podcast episode]. In *Craig Groeschel Leadership Podcast*. Life.Church. Retrieved from https://open.life.church/training/315-craig-groeschel-leadership-podcast-how-to-develop-leaders

68. Top Companies Leverage Internal Social Networks - Workology. https://workology.com/top-companies-leverage-internal-social-networks/

69. Hemingway, E. (n.d.). *Across the River and Into the Trees*.

70. Covey, S. R. (1989). *The 7 habits of highly effective people: Powerful lessons in personal change*. Free Press

71. Tracy, B. (n.d.). *The power of pausing*. Brian Tracy International. Retrieved from https://www.briantracy.com/blog/sales-success/the-power-of-pausing/

72. Anonymous. (n.d.). "Silence isn't empty. It's full of answers."

73. Drucker, P. F. (1989). Interview with Bill Moyers. In *A World of Ideas* [Television series]. Public Affairs Television.

74. Gates, B. (2013, April). *Bill Gates: Teachers need real feedback* [Video]. TED Conferences. https://www.ted.com/talks/bill_gates_teachers_need_real_feedback

75. The Muse. (n.d.). *Destructive vs. constructive criticism at work (with examples)*. The Muse. Retrieved from https://www.themuse.com/advice/destructive-vs-constructive-criticism-at-work-examples

76. Center for Creative Leadership. (2022, November 18). *Use Situation-Behavior-Impact (SBI)™ to Understand Intent.* https://www.ccl.org/articles/leading-effectively-articles/closing-the-gap-between-intent-vs-impact-sbii/

77. Scott, K. (2019). *Radical candor: Be a kick-ass boss without losing your humanity* (Revised & updated ed.). St. Martin's Publishing Group.

78. Hastings, R., & Meyer, E. (2020). *No rules rules: Netflix and the culture of reinvention.* Penguin Press.

79. McCord, P. (2018). *Powerful: Building a Culture of Freedom and Responsibility.* Silicon Guild.

80. Beahm, G. (2011). *I, Steve: Steve Jobs in His Own Words.* Agate Publishing.

81. Roffey Park. (n.d.). Managing vs coaching in the workplace: What is the difference? Retrieved April 1, 2025, from https://www.roffeypark.com/articles/what-is-the-difference-between-managing-and-coaching-in-the-workplace/

82. BrainyQuote. (n.d.). Jack Welch Quotes. Retrieved April 1, 2025, from https://www.brainyquote.com/quotes/jack_welch_833427

83. Whitmore, J. (1992). *Coaching for Performance: GROWing Human Potential and Purpose.* Nicholas Brealey Publishing

84. How to structure a good 1:1 conversation: the conversation funnel. https://www.openblend.com/blog/how-to-structure-a-good-conversation-the-conversation-funnel

85. Schmidt, E., Rosenberg, J., & Eagle, A. (2019). *Trillion Dollar Coach: The Leadership Playbook of Silicon Valley's Bill Campbell*. Harper Business.

86. Sinek, S. (2009). *Start with Why: How Great Leaders Inspire Everyone to Take Action*. Portfolio.

87. Whitmore, J. (2017). *Coaching for performance: The principles and practice of coaching and leadership* (5th ed.). Nicholas Brealey Publishing.

88. Anonymous. (n.d.). "People don't grow when they're told what to do. They grow when they're challenged, encouraged, and supported."

89. Ken Blanchard quote: The key to successful leadership today is influence, not authority.. https://www.azquotes.com/quote/519393?ref=strategic-management

90. Buffett, W. E. (2024). *2024 Annual Letter to Shareholders*. Berkshire Hathaway Inc. Retrieved from https://www.berkshirehathaway.com/letters/2024ltr.pdf

91. Mahnot, S. (2025, March 25). *What makes Oprah Winfrey a great leader? Emotional intelligence.* LinkedIn. Retrieved April 2, 2025, from https://www.linkedin.com/pulse/what-makes-oprah-winfrey-great-leader-emotional-surbhi-mahnot-1lkzc

92. Cialdini, R. B. (2006). *Influence: The psychology of persuasion* (Revised ed.). Harper Business

93. Isaacson, W. (2011). *Steve Jobs*. Simon & Schuster.

94. Anand, Y. P. (n.d.). Mahatma Gandhi's leadership—Moral and spiritual foundations. *Mahatma Gandhi Foundation*. Retrieved April 2, 2025, from https://www.mkgandhi.org/articles/sept081.php

95. WHY DID THE BRITISH COLONIES FIGHT. https://godsempires.com/why-did-the-british-colonies-fight-l-en/

96. Influencing Without Authority – Business Performance Specialists | Better Your Best. https://www.betteryourbest.ca/2021/10/influencing-without-authority/

97. Reagan, R. (1982, May 9). *Commencement Address at Eureka College*. Eureka College, Eureka, IL. Retrieved from https://www.reaganfoundation.org/ronald-reagan/quotes/peace-is-not-the-absence-of-conflict-but-the-ability

98. Teamwork in Organizations – Foundations of Commerce. https://pressbooks.library.virginia.edu/foundationsofcommerce/chapter/teamwork/

99. Sinek, S. (2024, July 15). The single best way to peacefully resolve conflicts at work. *Simon Sinek's Blog*. https://simonsinek.com/stories/one-thing-you-have-to-do-when-resolving-conflict-at-work/

100. Ohno, T. (1988). *Toyota production system: Beyond large-scale production*. Productivity Press

101. How to Shift from Selling Products to Selling Services - The Radix Group. https://theradixgroupllc.com/how-to-shift-from-selling-products-to-selling-services/

102. Stillman, J. (2018, May 4). The 1 book that transformed Microsoft's culture from cutthroat to creative. *Inc.* https://www.inc.com/jessica-stillman/this-1-book-that-transformed-microsofts-culture-from-cutthroat-to-creative.html

103. Brown, B. (2018, October 15). Clear is kind. Unclear is unkind. *Brené Brown's Blog.* https://brenebrown.com/articles/2018/10/15/clear-is-kind-unclear-is-unkind/

104. King, M. L., Jr. (1963, August 28). *I have a dream.* Speech presented at the March on Washington for Jobs and Freedom, Washington, D.C. Retrieved from https://www.britannica.com/topic/I-Have-A-Dream

105. Gallo, C. (2010). *The presentation secrets of Steve Jobs: How to be insanely great in front of any audience.* McGraw-Hill Education.

106. Jobs, S. (2001, October 23). *Apple iPod unveiling.* Apple Special Event, Cupertino, CA. Retrieved from https://www.cultofmac.com/news/today-in-apple-history-apple-puts-1000-songs-in-your-pocket-with-first-gen-ipod

107. Jobs, S. (2007, January 9). *Macworld Conference & Expo keynote address.* San Francisco, CA. Retrieved from https://www.apple.com/newsroom/2007/01/09Apple-Reinvents-the-Phone-with-iPhone/

108. Jobs, S. (2005, June 12). *Stanford University commencement address.* Stanford University, CA

109. Xmind. (2023, March 27). The Rule of Three: Boost Audience Retention in Presentations. *Xmind Blog.* https://xmind.app/blog/the-rule-of-three/

110. Gruenert, S., & Whitaker, T. (2015). *School culture rewired: How to define, assess, and transform it.* ASCD.

111. Burkus, D. (2020, April 28). How Paul O'Neill fought for safety at Alcoa. *David Burkus.* https://davidburkus.com/2020/04/how-paul-oneill-fought-for-safety-at-alcoa/

112. Robert Half. (n.d.). Creating a strong learning culture. Robert Half. Retrieved from https://www.roberthalf.com/blog/management-tips/creating-a-strong-learning-culture

113. O.C. Tanner. (n.d.). The impact of company culture on employees. O.C. Tanner Institute. Retrieved from https://www.octanner.com/insights/articles/2020/5/26/the_impact_of_compa.html

114. Kotter, J. P., & Heskett, J. L. (1992). *Corporate culture and performance.* Free Press.

115. Harbert College of Business. (2020). *Zappos finds the perfect fit.* Auburn University Center for Ethical Organizational Cultures. https://harbert.auburn.edu/binaries/documents/center-for-ethical-organizational-cultures/cases/zappos.pdf

116. Google. (n.d.). *Guides: Understand team effectiveness.* re:Work. https://rework.withgoogle.com/en/guides/understanding-team-effectiveness

117. Hsieh, T. (2010). *Delivering happiness: A path to profits, passion, and purpose.* Business Plus.

118. African Proverb. (n.d.). *If you want to go fast, go alone. If you want to go far, go together.*

119. Crisis Management Plans: 5 Key Behaviors for Success - Yieldify. https://www.yieldify.com/blog/crisis-management-plan/

120. General George S Patton Jr. - by Phin Barnes. https://www.sneakerheadvc.com/p/general-george-s-patton-jr-e9e3238fe56b

121. Branson, R. (2014, October 27). *You learn by doing and by falling over*. Virgin. https://www.virgin.com/branson-family/richard-branson-blog/you-learn-by-doing-and-by-falling-over

122. Hamada, K. (2023, September 15). *6 practical steps for effective delegation*. Khalid Hamada. https://khalidhamada.com/6-practical-steps-for-effective-delegation/

123. Reyes, J. (2023, December 21). *The 5W1H method: Elements & example*. SafetyCulture. https://safetyculture.com/topics/5w1h/

124. Nader, R. (n.d.). *The function of leadership is to produce more leaders, not more followers.*

125. Gandhi, M. (n.d.). *The best way to find yourself is to lose yourself in the service of others.*

126. Behar, H. (n.d.). *We're not in the coffee business serving people; we're in the people business serving coffee.*

127. Munn, B. (2020, October 12). *Nelson Mandela's servant leadership: What we can learn from him*. Bill Munn Coaching. https://billmunncoaching.com/nelson-mandela-servant-leader/

128.When I Work. (2023, August 20). *The ultimate guide to the servant leadership model*. When I Work Blog. https://wheniwork.com/blog/the-ultimate-guide-to-the-serv ant-leadership-model

129.Maxwell, J. C. (1993). *Developing the leader within you*. Thomas Nelson.

130.People work for money but go the extra mile for recognition – Brownie Points. https://browniepoints.com.au/people-work-for-money-but-go-the-extra-mile-for-recognition/

131.Conant, D. (2022, April 28). *During my tenure at Campbell Soup company, I wrote over 30,000 notes of thanks to employees within the organization* [LinkedIn post]. LinkedIn. https://www.linkedin.com/posts/dougconant_during-my-te nure-at-campbell-soup-company-activity-69345710322928 35328-s66g

132.Grant, A. M., & Gino, F. (2010). A little thanks goes a long way: Explaining why gratitude expressions motivate prosocial behavior. *Journal of Personality and Social Psychology*, 98(6), 946–955. https://doi.org/10.1037/a0017935

133.Glassdoor Team. (2017, April 12). Thanks but no thanks: Survey reveals strangest forms of workplace recognition. Glassdoor. https://press.roberthalf.com/2017-04-12-THANKS-BUT-NO-THANKS-Survey-Reveals-Strangest-Forms-of-Workplace-Rec ognition-Research-Also-Finds-Two-in-Three-Employees-Wo uld-Leave-Their-Job-If-They-Didnt-Feel-Appreciated

134. Gallup. (2016, June 28). The importance of employee recognition: Low cost, high impact. Gallup Workplace. https://www.gallup.com/workplace/236441/employee-reco gnition-low-cost-high-impact.aspx

135. William James | d-un zero. https://d-10.ro/quote-authors/william-james/

136. Shinseki, E. K. (2001, December 10). *Marines Turned Soldiers*. National Review Online. https://www.nationalreview.com/2001/12/marines-turned-soldiers-mackubin-thomas-owens/

137. The future of micromobility: Ridership and revenue after a crisis | McKinsey. https://www.mckinsey.com/industries/automotive-and-ass embly/our-insights/the-future-of-micromobility-ridership-a nd-revenue-after-a-crisis?cid=other-eml-alt-mip-mck&hlkid =5a6444a593534d0b8ea1190a39e6c713&hctky=10258153 &hdpid=24d62c73-cb52-4342-a0e4-94db9d09f2f8

138. Olson, P. (2017, September 19). How Toys 'R' Us neglected the web. *Forbes*. https://www.forbes.com/sites/parmyolson/2017/09/19/toys -r-us-chapter-11-amazon/

139. Weller, C. (2016, February 4). Remember when Yahoo turned down $1 million to buy Google? *Yahoo Finance*. https://finance.yahoo.com/news/remember-yahoo-turned-down-1-132805083.html

140. Lamberg, J.-A., Lubinaité, S., Ojala, J., & Tikkanen, H. (2021). The curse of agility: The Nokia Corporation and the loss of market dominance in mobile phones, 2003–2013. *Business History*, 63(4), 569–605. https://doi.org/10.1080/00076791.2019.1593964

141.Chesky, B. (2020, May 5). A message from co-founder and CEO Brian Chesky. *Airbnb Newsroom*. https://news.airbnb.com/a-message-from-co-founder-and-ceo-brian-chesky/

142.Yohn, D. L. (2020, November 10). How Airbnb survived the pandemic—and how you can too. *Forbes*. https://www.forbes.com/sites/deniselyohn/2020/11/10/how-airbnb-survived-the-pandemic--and-how-you-can-too/

143.Chesky, B. (2022, March 1). Brian Chesky on managing through crisis and uncertainty. *Stanford Graduate School of Business*. https://www.gsb.stanford.edu/insights/brian-chesky-managing-through-crisis-uncertainty

144.Army University Press. (2025, March). Understanding adaptive leadership. *NCO Journal*. https://www.armyupress.army.mil/Journals/NCO-Journal/Archives/2025/March/Understanding-Adaptive-Leadership/

145.Dweck, C. S. (2016). *Mindset: The New Psychology of Success*. Random House.

146.Buscaglia, L. (1972). *Love*. Fawcett.

147.Doidge, N. (2007). *The brain that changes itself: Stories of personal triumph from the frontiers of brain science*. Viking.

148.Saxena, J. (2021, May 24). There is no 'after' the reckoning for restaurants. *Eater*. https://www.eater.com/22446430/restaurant-reckoning-summer-2020-social-justice-result-fat-rice

149.Toffler, A. (1970). *Future Shock*. Random House.

150. Brooks, P. (1905). *Christ the Life and Light: Lenten Readings.* E.P. Dutton.

151. Britannica. (n.d.). *US Airways flight 1549 incident.* https://www.britannica.com/topic/US-Airways-Flight-1549-incident

152. Emotional intelligence in leadership: A key to building resilient teams. (n.d.). *International Journal of Academic Research in Business and Social Sciences,* 11(2), 20-35. https://www.researchgate.net/publication/387705289_Emotional_Intelligence_in_Leadership_A_Key_to_Building_Resilient_Teams

153. Adapt or die: Leadership resilience during crisis. (2022). *International Journal of Advanced Corporate Learning,* 15(2), 4-15. https://online-journals.org/index.php/i-jac/article/view/30683

154. Optimism: A leadership superpower. (n.d.). *Association of Executive Search and Leadership Consultants.* https://www.aesc.org/insights/magazine/article/optimism-leadership-superpower

155. The role of resilience in leadership and culture. (n.d.). *American Association of School Administrators.* https://www.aasa.org/docs/default-source/resources/reports/the-role-of-resiliency-in-leadership-and-culture.pdf

156. Healthline. (n.d.). *10 breathing techniques for stress relief.* https://www.healthline.com/health/breathing-exercise

157. Barker, E. (2017). *How to be calm under pressure: 3 secrets from a bomb disposal expert.* https://bakadesuyo.com/2017/01/calm-under-pressure/

158. Barker, E. (2017). *How to be calm under pressure: 3 secrets from a bomb disposal expert.* https://bakadesuyo.com/2017/01/calm-under-pressure/

159. Harvard Business Review. (2019, July). *Life's Work: An Interview with Vera Wang.* https://hbr.org/2019/07/lifes-work-an-interview-with-vera-wang

160. Quotefancy. (n.d.). *Top 60 Vera Wang Quotes (2025 Update).* https://quotefancy.com/vera-wang-quotes

161. Markus, C., McFeely, S., & Petroni, M. (Screenwriters). (2010). *The Chronicles of Narnia: The Voyage of the Dawn Treader* [Film]. 20th Century Fox

162. Master Communication & Strategic Thinking Courses 2025. https://www.arthsetu.com/courses

163. Wikipedia contributors. (2025, March 28). *Deep Blue versus Garry Kasparov.* Wikipedia, The Free Encyclopedia. https://en.wikipedia.org/wiki/Deep_Blue_versus_Garry_Kasparov

164. Tartakower, S. (n.d.). *Quotations.* Retrieved April 4, 2025, from https://en.wikipedia.org/wiki/Savielly_Tartakower

165. Schoemaker, P. J. H. (1995). *Scenario planning: A tool for strategic thinking.* MIT Sloan Management Review, 36(2), 25–40. https://sloanreview.mit.edu/article/scenario-planning-a-tool-for-strategic-thinking/

166. Martin, R. (2011, March). *Managing yourself: Zoom in, zoom out.* Harvard Business Review. https://hbr.org/2011/03/managing-yourself-zoom-in-zoom-out

167. Impact Leadership Team. (2024, May 15). *Avoiding groupthink: The power of red teaming.* https://www.impactleadershipteam.com/2024/05/15/avoiding-groupthink-the-power-of-red-teaming/

168. Unknown. (n.d.). Strategy without reflection is just luck.

169. Britannica. (n.d.). *Euro-zone debt crisis.* https://www.britannica.com/money/euro-zone-debt-crisis

170. Harvard Kennedy School. (n.d.). *Wir schaffen das: Angela Merkel and Germany's response to the refugee crisis in Europe.* https://case.hks.harvard.edu/wir-schaffen-das-angela-merkel-and-germanys-response-to-the-refugee-crisis-in-europe/

171. German Marshall Fund of the United States. (n.d.). *COVID-19 has democratic lessons to teach. Has Angela Merkel helped Germany learn them?.* https://www.gmfus.org/news/covid-19-has-democratic-lessons-teach-has-angela-merkel-helped-germany-learn-them

172. Anonymous. (n.d.). *Failing to plan is planning to fail.*

173. Edmondson, A. (n.d.). *Creating Psychological Safety in the Workplace.* University of California, Berkeley. Retrieved April 5, 2025, from https://hr.berkeley.edu/creating-psychological-safety-workplace

174. Edmondson, A. C. (1999). Psychological safety and learning behavior in work teams. *Administrative Science Quarterly, 44*(2), 350–383. https://doi.org/10.2307/2666999

175. Duhigg, C. (2016, February 25). *What Google Learned From Its Quest to Build the Perfect Team.* The New York Times. https://www.nytimes.com/2016/02/28/magazine/what-google-learned-from-its-quest-to-build-the-perfect-team.html

233

176. Rozovsky, J. (n.d.). *Guide: Understand team effectiveness.* Google re:Work. Retrieved April 5, 2025, from https://rework.withgoogle.com/en/guides/understanding-team-effectiveness

177. Brown, B. (2012). *Daring greatly: How the courage to be vulnerable transforms the way we live, love, parent, and lead.* Gotham Books.

178. National Aeronautics and Space Administration. (1986). *Report of the Presidential Commission on the Space Shuttle Challenger Accident.* Washington, DC: U.S. Government Printing Office

179. #3FastFacts: Resilience at Scale - Do Change Right. https://dochangeright.com/3fastfacts-resilience-at-scale/

180. Stanley, A. [@AndyStanley]. (2021, August 19). *Leaders who don't listen will eventually be surrounded by people who have nothing to say.* [Tweet]. Twitter. https://x.com/AndyStanley/status/1428471840603885577

181. Mehta, S. (2024, May 20). Satya Nadella transformed Microsoft's culture during his decade as CEO by turning everyone into 'learn-it-alls' instead of 'know-it-alls'. *Fortune.* https://fortune.com/2024/05/20/satya-nadella-microsoft-culture-growth-mindset-learn-it-alls-know-it-alls/

182. Catmull, E. (2008). How Pixar fosters collective creativity. *Harvard Business Review.* https://hbr.org/2008/09/how-pixar-fosters-collective-creativity

183. Loehr, J., & Schwartz, T. (2003). *The power of full engagement: Managing energy, not time, is the key to high performance and personal renewal.* Free Press.

184. Groeschel, C. (Host). (2019, July 1). *Understanding your four forms of energy* (No. 57) [Audio podcast episode]. In *Craig Groeschel Leadership Podcast*. Life.Church. https://www.life.church/leadershippodcast/leadership/und erstanding-your-four-forms-of-energy/

185. Branson, R. (2017, November 30). *My morning routine*. Virgin. https://www.virgin.com/branson-family/richard-branson-bl og/my-morning-routine

186. Newport, C. (2016). *Deep work: Rules for focused success in a distracted world*. Grand Central Publishing.

187. Articles | Authentic Achievements. https://authenticachievements.com/category/authentic-ach ievements-latest-news/page/2/

188. Musk, E. (2017). *Making life multiplanetary* [Conference presentation]. International Astronautical Congress, Adelaide, Australia. https://www.spacex.com/media/making_life_multiplanetary _transcript_2017.pdf

189. Clear, J. (2012, December 19). Plan for failure: Being consistent is not the same as being perfect. James Clear. https://jamesclear.com/plan-failure

190. Huffington, A. (2017, April 6). 10 years ago I collapsed from burnout and exhaustion, and it's the best thing that could have happened to me. *Thrive Global*. https://medium.com/thrive-global/10-years-ago-i-collapsed -from-burnout-and-exhaustion-and-its-the-best-thing-that- could-have-b1409f16585d

191. AlertMedia. (2024, August 17). *The 4 stages of crisis and how to manage them*. AlertMedia. https://www.alertmedia.com/blog/stages-of-crisis/

192. Holtom, B., Edmondson, A. C., & Niu, D. (2020, July 9). *5 tips for communicating with employees during a crisis*. Harvard Business Review. https://hbr.org/2020/07/5-tips-for-communicating-with-employees-during-a-crisis

193. Solv Communications. (2023, September 15). *The ultimate crisis management plan [The PR playbook]*. Solv Communications. https://solvcommunications.ca/crisis-communications-plan-template/

194. Shorrock, S. (2019). QF32: How it went right. *Skybrary*.

195. Brown, B. (2018, October 15). Clear Is Kind. Unclear Is Unkind. *Brené Brown*. https://brenebrown.com/articles/2018/10/15/clear-is-kind-unclear-is-unkind/

196. Communication Theory. (n.d.). *The 7 C's of Effective Communication – Explained with Examples*. Communication Theory. Retrieved April 5, 2025, from https://www.communicationtheory.org/the-7cs-of-effective-communication-explained-with-examples/

197. Voss, C. (2023, February 15). *FBI negotiation techniques: Mirror & label*. YouTube. https://www.youtube.com/watch?v=vZTjgaDa-fU

198. Gabler, N. (2006). *Walt Disney: The triumph of the American imagination*. Alfred A. Knopf.

199. The Art of Storytelling in Content Marketing: Engaging Your Audience | Contentscape. https://contentscape.co.uk/the-art-of-storytelling-in-content-marketing-engaging-your-audience/

200. Ferrazzi, K. [@keithferrazzi]. (2023, October 25). *Embracing the power of storytelling! I've learned that diving deep into personal stories is not just an option; it's a MUST in any speech* [Video]. Instagram. https://www.instagram.com/reel/Cy1YL2Nq-PT/

201. Heath, C., & Heath, D. (2007). *Made to stick: Why some ideas survive and others die*. Random House.

202. Campbell, J. (2008). *The hero with a thousand faces* (3rd ed.). New World Library. (Original work published 1949)

203. Massachusetts Institute of Technology. (1998, April 8). *Body Shop founder discusses principles*. MIT News. https://news.mit.edu/1998/bodyshop-0408

204. McKee, R. (n.d.). *Quotes*. IMDb. https://www.imdb.com/name/nm0571210/quotes/

205. OpenAI. (2025). *Impact Audit: Leadership dimensions and long-term influence*. ChatGPT. https://chat.openai.com

206. OpenAI. (2025, April 6). *The 4 key components of a lasting leadership legacy* [Text generated by ChatGPT]. OpenAI.

207. Schein, E. H. (2020). *Fred Rogers—Building a leadership legacy based on kindness and authenticity*. In *Leadership and legacy: Inspiring others through kindness and authenticity* (pp. 102-104). Leadership Press.

208. Cory Booker Quote: "Leadership is not a position or a title, it is action and example.". https://quotefancy.com/quote/1099956/Cory-Booker-Leadership-is-not-a-position-or-a-title-it-is-action-and-example

209. ChatGPT. (2025). *The Growth Loop: Learn, Apply, Reflect, Adjust, Repeat*. In *Leadership Development: A Continuous Growth Process*. OpenAI.

210. Northouse, P. G. (2018). *Leadership: Theory and practice* (8th ed.). Sage Publications.

211. Locke, E. A., & Latham, G. P. (2002). *Building a practically useful theory of goal setting and task motivation*. American Psychologist, 57(9), 705–717. https://doi.org/10.1037/0003-066X.57.9.705

212. Kotter, J. P. (2012). *Leading change*. Harvard Business Review Press.

213. George, B. (2007). *True north: Discover your authentic leadership*. Jossey-Bass.

214. Schön, D. A. (1983). *The reflective practitioner: How professionals think in action*. Basic Books.

215. Huffington, A. (2016). *Thrive: The third metric to redefining success and creating a life of well-being, wisdom, and wonder*. Harmony.

216. Huffington, A. (2016). *Thrive: The third metric to redefining success and creating a life of well-being, wisdom, and wonder*. Harmony.